W9-BLV-398

New Zealand

New Zealand

BY DONNA WALSH SHEPHERD

Enchantment of the World™
Second Series

CHILDREN'S PRESS®

An Imprint of Scholastic Inc.

Frontispiece: **Mount Cook National Park**

Dedication: For Morrie Shepherd, my companion traveling the Land of the Long White Cloud

Acknowledgments: It is with deep appreciation that I thank New Zealanders Diane Woolson Neville, Mike Anstett, and Jill Smythe. I know they must have gotten tired of opening their e-mail and seeing my name with new questions. They kindly and generously shared their knowledge of New Zealand life with me. And thanks, too, to the Alexander Turnbull Library in New Zealand, which so thoroughly answered my questions and sent many useful links. And a special thank you to E. Russell Primm and Allison Henderson for their kindness, support, and patience.

Consultant: Professor Tom Brooking, History Department, University of Otago, Dunedin, New Zealand

Please note: All statistics are as up-to-date as possible at the time of publication.

Book production by The Design Lab

Library of Congress Cataloging-in-Publication Data
Walsh Shepherd, Donna.
New Zealand / by Donna Walsh Shepherd.
   pages cm. — (Enchantment of the world)
Includes bibliographical references and index.
ISBN 978-0-531-23296-5 (library binding)
1. New Zealand—Juvenile literature. I. Title.
DU408.W352 2016
993—dc23   2015026855

1 2 3 4 5 6 7 8 9 10 R 25 24 23 22 21 20 19 18 17 16

Maori carvings and the Sky Tower, Auckland

Contents

Left to right:
**Remarkables
mountain range,
kakapo, Maori,
sheep, yacht race**

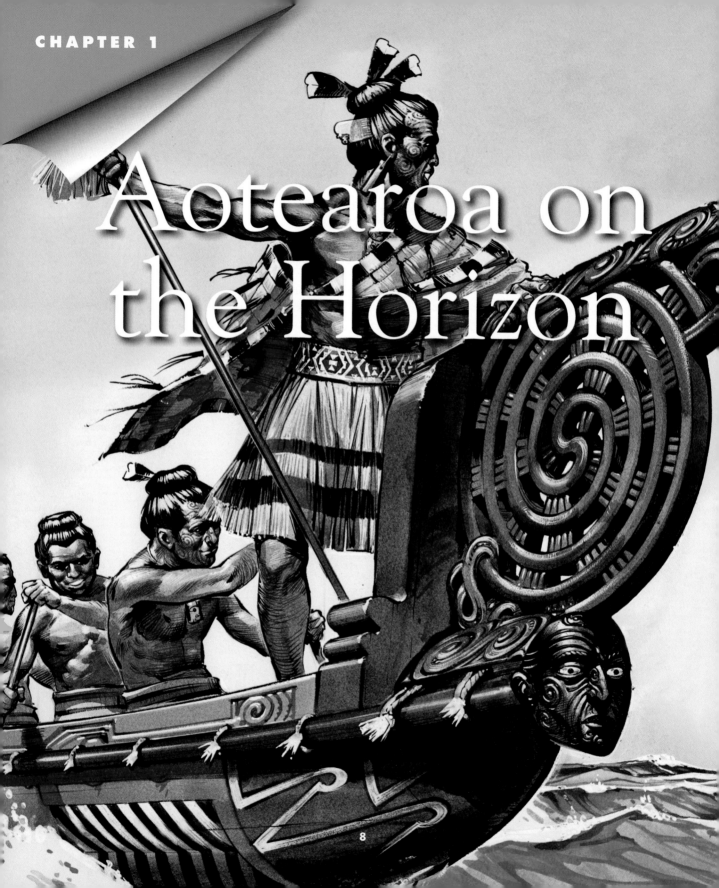

CHAPTER 1

Aotearoa on the Horizon

FOR MANY WEEKS, THE *WAKA*, THE LARGE CANOE, had been at sea. Together the men pulled stroke after stroke against the waves with large wooden paddles, some carved like leaves. The women trailed fishing lines behind the boat. Nestled around the men, women, and children were containers of water and leaf-wrapped packages of dried fruits, vegetables, and seeds. The seeds would help them start a new life in a distant place to the south. Many of their Polynesian relatives lived on islands scattered across the Pacific, but the time had come for this group to find a new home. So now they pulled together, stroke after stroke, heading south across the South Pacific Ocean.

They knew the legends of the great Polynesian explorer, Kupe. Generations earlier he and his crew had paddled far to the south, farther than any Polynesian (or European) had ever traveled. One day Kupe saw on the horizon a long, low white

Opposite: **The canoes of the Maori, the Polynesians who settled in New Zealand, are often elaborately decorated.**

Aotearoa on the Horizon   **9**

cloud. He knew that such a cloud would be caught on tops of mountains. Large mountains hooked the clouds and pulled them over the land. He named the land Aotearoa, Land of the Long White Cloud.

It was about the year 1280 CE when the people in the canoe set out to find the fabled land that Kupe had talked about upon his return. After many weeks of paddling, of stinging storms and blazing sun, one golden morning the foggy haze on the horizon

Clouds hang over the Southern Alps, a mountain range on New Zealand's South Island.

looked different. Bigger. Fuller. As the paddle strokes added up and the morning brightened into day, the people in the canoe saw a white heaviness stretching along the horizon. Generations of experience and knowledge speeded their paddles. They knew that under that long white cloud lay land.

As the group drew near to the land, they could see it was a bountiful area. Fish filled the water. Porpoises played alongside the canoe. The land was covered in lush jungle, and all around they heard the songs and squawks of birds. They waited, but no enemies came to meet them. It was a good land indeed.

The Polynesians stayed and thrived. They became known as the Maori, a word meaning "the normal ones." Soon, more

Traditional Maori oceangoing canoes were large. They often had dozens of paddlers.

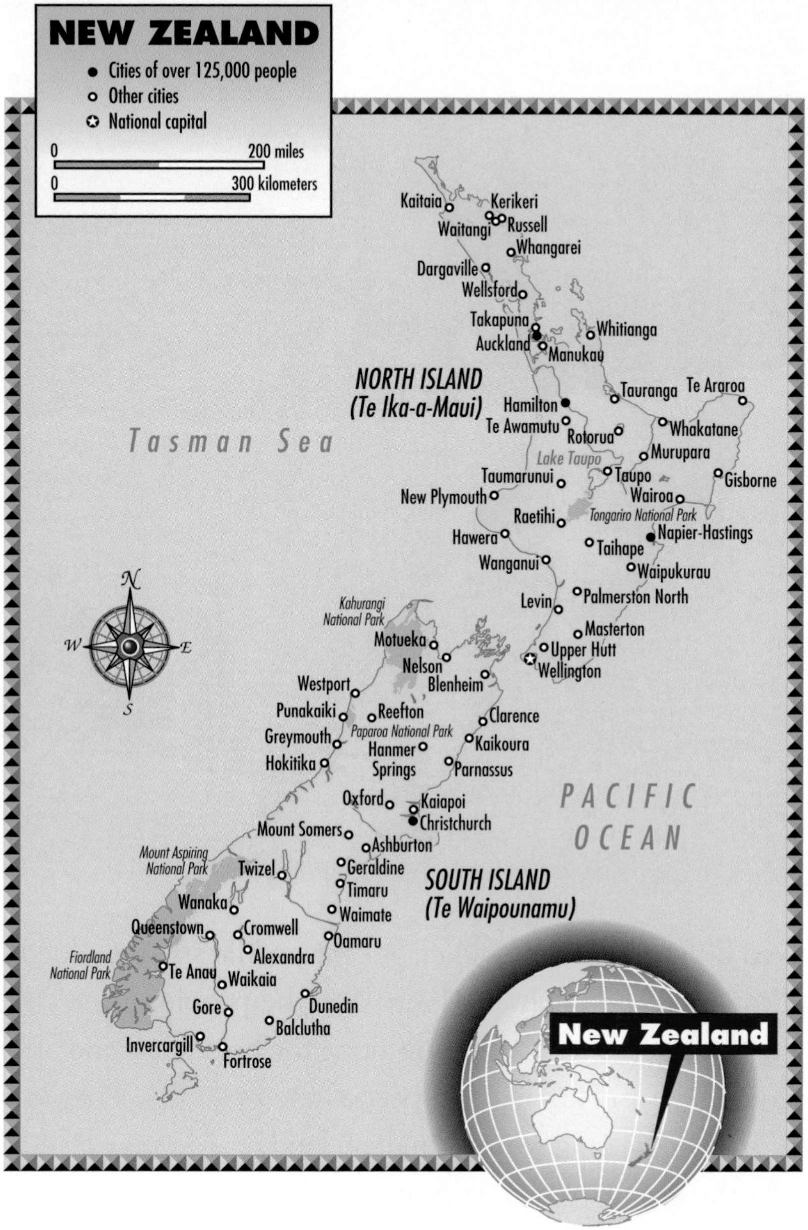
NEW ZEALAND
● Cities of over 125,000 people
○ Other cities
✪ National capital
0
200 miles
0
300 kilometers
Kaitaia
Kerikeri
Waitangi
Russell
Whangarei
Dargaville
Wellsford
Takapuna
Auckland
Manukau
Whitianga
NORTH ISLAND
(Te Ika-a-Maui)
Hamilton
Te Awamutu
Tauranga
Te Araroa
Rotorua
Whakatane
Tasman Sea
Lake Taupo
Murupara
Taumarunui
Taupo
Gisborne
New Plymouth
Wairoa
Raetihi
Tongariro National Park
Napier-Hastings
Hawera
Taihape
Wanganui
Waipukurau
N
W
E
S
Kahurangi
National Park
Levin
Palmerston North
Masterton
Motueka
Upper Hutt
Nelson
Wellington
Blenheim
Westport
Punakaiki
Reefton
Clarence
Paparoa National Park
Greymouth
Kaikoura
Hanmer
Springs
Hokitika
Parnassus
PACIFIC
OCEAN
Oxford
Kaiapoi
Christchurch
Mount Somers
Ashburton
Mount Aspiring
National Park
Twizel
Geraldine
SOUTH ISLAND
(Te Waipounamu)
Timaru
Wanaka
Waimate
Queenstown
Cromwell
Oamaru
Alexandra
Fiordland
National Park
Te Anau
Waikaia
Dunedin
Gore
Balclutha
Invercargill
Fortrose
New Zealand

canoes followed with more families to settle in Aotearoa. But as the centuries passed, there came a time when they did not have the islands to themselves. First the Dutch, then the English, and after that, people from all over the world came to the Land of the Long White Cloud.

New Adventurers

In 2015, a different boat enters a harbor on Aotearoa. This boat is also crowded with people eager to see the new land. At sea, they had seen Kupe's long white cloud hanging over the land. But in the harbor, the land looks very different from when the Maori first arrived. The Maori sailed into a bay that was empty except for birds and fish. These new explorers line the railing of a large cruise ship. They sail past cargo ships, tugboats, sailboats, tour boats, and fishing boats.

Boats are anchored in the water of Waitemata Harbour. It is one of two large harbors in Auckland, New Zealand's largest city.

From the railing the new visitors stare at the land. It is crowded not with jungle, but with skyscrapers, and beautiful homes on the hills. On the wharf at the water's edge, people walk along laughing, eating, and listening to music. Some sit on benches or lean against the rails and point and wave to the gleaming white cruise liner coming into the harbor. "*Kia ora! Kia ora!*"—Hello!—they call in greeting. The people on the ship wave back and know they are looking at a good land, a land of friendship and prosperity.

Many houses have been built in the green hills that rise from the coast in Wellington, the capital of New Zealand.

New Zealand Before Us

Beyond the cities and the orchards, past the cattle and sheep ranches, above the award-winning vineyards, there is still some of that thick forest the Maori first found. National parks and protected land cover more than 30 percent of New Zealand. Some of the creatures that first greeted the Maori, like the moa, a bird that looks like a giant ostrich, have disappeared. But penguins still swim in from the sea to nest on land. Whales still feed in the nearby waters, and fish still school in the currents. Volcanoes still occasionally erupt, and the earth occasionally quakes. And with that same furious sense of Maori adventure, people still come to Aotearoa, to New Zealand, to have fun, to explore a place unique in the world, or to build a new life. Kia Ora, New Zealand.

Hikers cross a bridge in the lush forests of Abel Tasman National Park. This park lies on the northern coast of the South Island.

CHAPTER 2

Remarkable Islands

ON THE SOUTH ISLAND, NEAR QUEENSTOWN, there is a range of mountains named the Remarkables. The jagged peaks rise steeply at the edge of a deep blue lake. It is so beautiful, so remarkable, many people smile in appreciation. "Remarkable" is a pretty good name for the geography of all New Zealand. Few countries can boast of such beauty and strangeness.

New Zealand is a long string of a country. It stretches from the warm subtropical north 1,000 miles (1,600 kilometers) to the cold south, where the wind blows storms in from Antarctica. Across those miles are meadows and marshes, long sandy beaches, coves and inlets, and high bluffs above the sea. New Zealand has bubbling hot mud pools, geysers, and blowholes. It even has rock formations that look like giant stacks of pancakes ready for ancient gods to swoop down and eat. And towering above it all are remarkable mountains.

Opposite: **The Remarkables rise abruptly from the edge of Lake Wakatipu. This jagged mountain range features popular ski areas.**

New Zealand's Geographic Features

Area: 104,454 square miles (270,535 sq km)

Length of Coastline: 9,404 miles (15,134 km)

Highest Elevation: Mount Cook, 12,218 feet (3,724 m) above sea level

Lowest Elevation: Sea level, along the coast

Highest Volcano: Ruapehu, 9,175 feet (2,797 m) above sea level

Largest Lake: Taupo, 234 square miles (606 sq km)

Longest River: Waikato, 264 miles (425 km)

Highest Waterfall: Sutherland Falls, 1,904 feet (580 m)

Biggest Glacier: Tasman, 38 square miles (98 sq km)

Average High Temperature: In Auckland, 74°F (23°C) in January, 59°F (15°C) in July

Average Low Temperature: In Auckland, 59°F (15°C) in January, 52°F (11°C) in July

Wettest Area: Southern Alps, 250 inches (635 cm) of precipitation per year

Dryest Area: Central Otago, 12 inches (30 cm) of precipitation per year

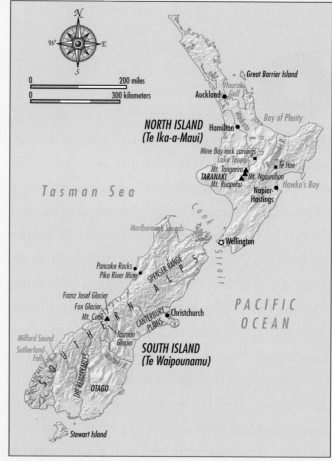

Alone at Sea

New Zealand is an island nation, so it does not share a border with any other nation. Although it has more than six hundred islands, there are two main ones: North Island, called Te Ika-a-Maui (the fish of Maui) in the Maori language, and South Island, or Te Waipounamu (greenstone waters). Many of the other islands are uninhabited.

New Zealand sits alone in the southwestern Pacific Ocean. Australia is nearly 1,200 miles (1,900 km) to the west across the Tasman Sea, which New Zealanders call the Ditch. South America lies 5,000 miles (8,000 km) to the east. Antarctica is 2,000 miles (3,200 km) farther south. Even its closest neighbors, the Oceanic countries of New Caledonia, Fiji, and Tonga are 600 miles (1,000 km) to the north. That isolation has given New Zealand a unique history and environment.

The Bay of Islands lies near the northeast coast of the North Island. The many islands in this bay were once hilltops overlooking valleys. When the ice melted at the end of the last ice age, sea levels rose, filling the valleys with water and turning the hills into islands.

Making Mountains

New Zealand sits on the southwestern edge of what is known as the Ring of Fire, an area of frequent volcanic activity. The Ring of Fire, which circles the Pacific Ocean, runs along boundaries between massive chunks of Earth's outer layer called tectonic plates. Along these meeting points, lava leaks through, forming volcanoes. Seventy-five percent of the volcanoes in the world are on the Ring of Fire. Sometimes lava oozes up through a vent, building a new landmass. The mountains of the North Island were formed this way.

Today there are many volcanoes on the North Island. Although most of New Zealand's volcanoes are dormant, one occasionally wakes up. In 2012, Mount Tongariro erupted for the first time in 115 years. Nearby Mount Ngauruhoe erupts far more frequently. During the 1900s, it erupted forty-five times. Offshore, deep in the Bay of Plenty over a hot spot on the ocean floor, lava is flowing upward, slowly building a new island for New Zealand.

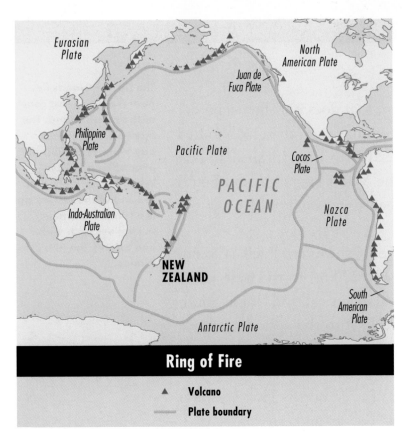

Ring of Fire

▲ Volcano

— Plate boundary

VAAC: Volcanic Ash Advisory Centers

One of nine ash-monitoring sites in the world is the Wellington Volcanic Ash Advisory Center (VAAC). There, scientists keep track of earthquakes and volcanic eruptions around the world. Volcanic ash is made of tiny sharp shards of minerals. Volcanic ash can damage car engines and people's lungs. It can also severely damage the engines of airplanes if they fly through it. The VAAC warns airplanes and airports around the world of eruptions and tells them which areas to avoid.

Ash billows into the sky during an eruption of Mount Tongariro in 2012.

The mountains of the South Island were formed differently. At the western edge of the South Island, two tectonic plates—the Pacific and the Indo-Australian—are pushing against each other. This is causing the Pacific Plate to buckle, creating ridges of tall mountain peaks. The Southern Alps and the Remarkables were formed this way. The land in the South Island is still being pushed up and out. The Southern Alps, the highest range in New Zealand, grow about 2 inches (5 centimeters) every five years, and the South Island widens by about an inch (2.5 cm) a year.

The highest peaks in the Southern Alps are covered in snow and ice throughout the year.

Mountain Shapes

Volcanic Mountains are often cone shaped and each stands alone. The mountain grows taller and wider with each new eruption. Mount Ruapehu in New Zealand and Mount Shasta in the United States are volcanic mountains.

Uplifted mountains form when one plate pushes against another causing the land to fold and buckle. Usually these mountains are long ridges of jagged peaks. The highest mountains around the world are uplifted mountains. The Southern Alps in New Zealand, the Rocky Mountains in North America, and the Himalayas in Asia are examples of uplifted mountain ranges.

As the South Island land was uplifted, great cracks emerged along the edges of the western coast. These steep-walled narrow inlets are called fjords. New Zealand has some of the most dramatic fjords in the world, including Milford Sound.

From the Mountains to the Sea

Many of the mountains in the Southern Alps are covered with glaciers, permanent sheets of ice. The largest, Tasman Glacier, lies on the eastern flank of Mount Cook, the nation's highest peak.

The mountains of the South Island are steep and rocky. But near the west coast, the land flattens out into the Canterbury Plains, much of which has been turned into farmland. A large plateau in the center of the North Island has become productive farmland and grazing land.

Wind, rain, and waves have eroded the rock near Punakaiki to form the stunning Pancake Rocks.

The coastline of New Zealand is varied. There are quiet beaches, sandy dunes, rugged cliffs, dramatic fjords, and many spectacular rock formations. Near Punakaiki on the South Island is a site called Pancake Rocks. Here, layers of soft and hard rock have created formations that look like stacks of pancakes.

Earthquakes

Both the North and South Islands experience earthquakes, but for different reasons. Often, before a volcano erupts there will be many small warning earthquakes called swarms. This happens as lava moves up through the mountain, or gases and ash build pressure and shift.

Other earthquakes occur when tectonic plates that are pushing against each other slip suddenly. These quakes can be devastating. In September 2010, an earthquake struck the region of Christchurch, weakening many of the city's structures. Then, on February 22, 2011, a second quake hit the area. The quake shook apart Christchurch, doing billions of dollars of damage and killing 185 people.

Once a community has experienced a tragedy like a big earthquake, people remain skittish. They look around nervously when they feel the first small vibrations. In January 2015, a 6.0 quake hit west of Christchurch. Little damage was done, but the shaking reminded everyone to update their eqnz. An eqnz is what New Zealanders call their emergency preparedness kit. Its name is short for "earthquake New Zealand." It's a good idea to have an eqnz when living on an earthquake fault surrounded by volcanoes.

Thousands of buildings in Christchurch collapsed in the 2011 earthquake.

Looking at New Zealand's Cities

With a population of nearly 1.5 million, Auckland (below) is New Zealand's largest city and the world's largest Polynesian community. Auckland is a beautiful city nestled between two harbors and surrounded by parkland and hiking trails. It is nicknamed the City of Sails because sailing is so popular in the region. Auckland is the financial and business center of New Zealand, and the site of the nation's main international airport and shipping hub. A unique mix of big-city sophistication and New Zealand fun, it has a growing tourist industry. People come for the vibrant music scene, the magnificent art at the Auckland Art Gallery, the many parks, and the delicious food.

Wellington, New Zealand's second-largest city with a population of about 400,000, is also its capital. Christchurch (above, right), the third-largest city with a

population of more than 380,000, is the New Zealand city that is most like Great Britain. British settlers founded it in 1850. They were homesick so they brought plants and animals to remind them of England. They built houses in a British style and planted traditional English gardens. They played games from home, like lawn bowling and cricket, and traveled on the river in British-style boats called punts. In the center of town, they built the magnificent Church of Christ Cathedral. Today, Christchurch is the most important business center and port on the South Island. The city is still recovering from the devastating earthquake of 2011 that destroyed 70 percent of the downtown business district, including the cathedral. A temporary replacement has been built for the cathedral, while other parts of the city have been rebuilt to better withstand earthquakes. Some parts of the city will never be rebuilt because they are on land that is now considered unsafe.

Hamilton, the nation's fourth-largest city, has a population of about 220,000. Located on the North Island, it is an agricultural center and the nation's major inland city. The city is home to both the University of Waikato and the Waikato Institute of Technology, and both education and research are important to its economy.

Rivers and Lakes

Swift rivers rush down from the mountains in New Zealand. The longest river is the Waikato, on the North Island. Dams have been built on many rivers in the western South Island, providing the nation with a great deal of hydroelectric power. This region's rivers also attract many raft and kayak adventurers. When some of these rivers reach the west coast, they cascade down the high cliffs of the fjords, creating huge waterfalls like the Sutherland Falls on Milford Sound.

Lakes on the South Island are mostly basin lakes. These are lakes that are filled by snowmelt and rain, rather than an underground water source. On the North Island, rain has filled ancient volcano craters to create deep lakes. Lake Taupo, New Zealand's largest lake, was created more than twenty-five thousand years ago when Mount Taupo erupted. That eruption was the world's largest in seventy thousand years.

Sutherland Falls is among the tallest waterfalls in New Zealand. It drops a total of 1,904 feet (580 m).

Seasons in Reverse

When the North Pole tips away from the sun, winter comes to North America. That time of the year, the Southern Hemisphere is angling toward the sun, so there it is summer. From December to February, while many North Americans are shoveling snow, New Zealanders are at the beach or sailing. And New Zealanders have to pull out winter jackets in June, July, and August.

In the Wet

While New Zealand's geography is varied, its climate is far less so. New Zealand stretches about the same distance as from the Canadian border to the Gulf of Mexico. However, New Zealand does not normally have the harsh winters of Canada or the sweltering summers of the Gulf Coast. The currents of the South Pacific Ocean and the Tasman Sea keep New Zealand's temperatures moderate, with highs of between 60 and 86 degrees Fahrenheit (16 and 30 degrees Celsius). The westerly winds normally carry ample rainfall. Sometimes the winds shift

Down the Drain

South of the equator water spins clockwise as it goes down the drain. North of the equator it spins counter-clockwise. This happens because Earth rotates east and gravity pulls the water toward Earth's center core. Hold a glass of water and stir it counterclockwise. Now hold the glass over your head as though you were in the Southern Hemisphere looking up at the equator. The water appears to be spinning clockwise.

and bring gales from Antarctica or warm tropical storms from the north. Then flooding in low areas can be a problem.

New Zealand rain is usually reliable, but how much falls varies widely depending on location and season. On the North Island more rain falls in the winter. On the South Island, rain comes more in summer storms. There, the Remarkables, the Southern Alps, and the Spenser Range act as a shower curtain keeping the rain on the west side of the country. Areas along the west coast can get more than 200 inches (500 cm) of rain a year, while areas on the Canterbury Plains receive about 11 inches (28 cm) a year.

Pedestrians cross the street on a wet day in Auckland, where rain is common throughout the year.

Warming and Shrinking

The changing weather patterns that are affecting much of the world are also affecting New Zealand. The winter of 2014 brought something new to the South Island: a winter with little snow. It was the warmest winter since record keeping began in 1909. It was so warm that if moisture came, it came as rain. The three largest ski resorts near Queenstown were able to open their season on time, though, using machine-made snow.

The warm weather is also having a disturbing effect on New Zealand's glaciers. Since 1976, two of New Zealand's most famous glaciers, Franz Josef Glacier and Fox Glacier, have melted back nearly 2 miles (3 km). The depth of the glaciers is also thinning. Scientists have determined that between 15 and 30 percent of the glaciers have been lost.

Snowfall is common in the higher altitudes of the mountains, especially on the South Island. There, the mountains are so rugged and the snow normally so abundant that elite skiers, snowboarders, and mountain climbers from the Northern Hemisphere come to train during their summer months.

National Parks and Forests

New Zealanders have worked hard to preserve their rich environment. In 1887, Maori leader Horonuku Te Heuheu presented a tract of land in central North Island to the British Crown to preserve for the people of New Zealand. This area became Tongariro National Park, New Zealand's first national park, in 1894. It includes the south shore of Lake Taupo, three volcanoes, and sacred Maori sites. The United Nations has named it a World Heritage Site, noted for both its extraordinary beauty and cultural importance.

Today, New Zealand has fourteen national parks, nineteen national forests, three maritime parks, and two marine parks. They cover environments from volcanic peaks to tide pool beaches. Fiordland National Park has spectacular cliffs and thundering waterfalls. Paparoa National Park is the perfect place to explore rugged canyons and caves.

Algae-covered boulders are exposed during low tide at Paparoa National Park.

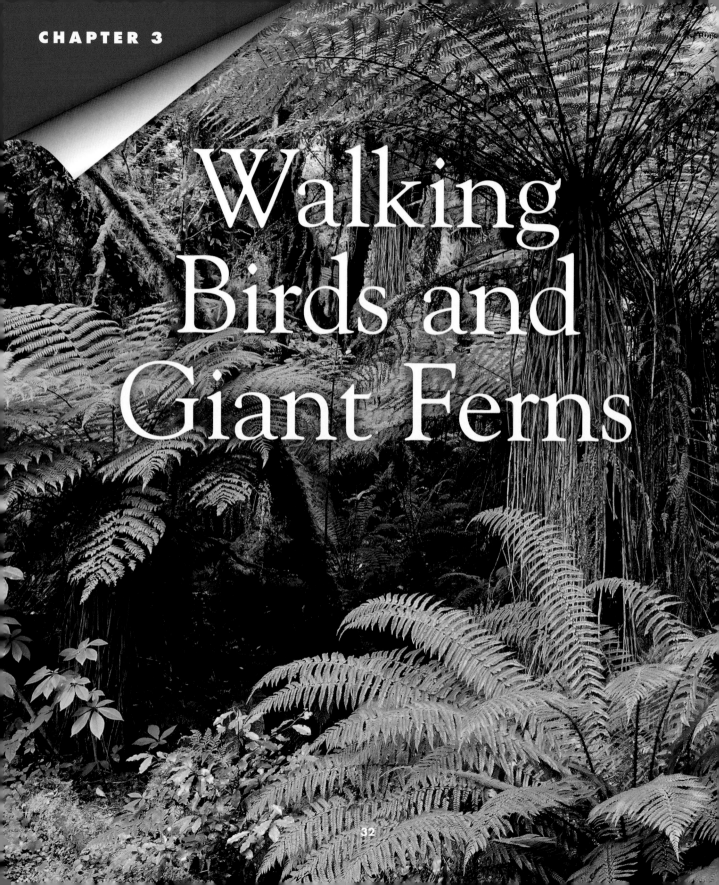

CHAPTER 3

Walking Birds and Giant Ferns

LIFE DEVELOPED DIFFERENTLY IN NEW ZEALAND than it did in other places that are not so isolated. Because New Zealand is so far out in the ocean, birds could fly there to live, but most predators could not get there. Plant life on the islands grew thick and lush; the forest hummed with insects. It was almost bird heaven. Bats, the only mammals on the islands, ate primarily insects, flowers, and fruit. When the trees dropped seeds to the ground, the birds happily scuffled along the forest floor eating their fill.

Without predators, it wasn't necessary for the birds to fly back up to the safety of the treetops. Gradually, many bird species lost their ability to fly. Some even lost their wings. But that didn't matter, they could walk to all the food they needed and build nests on the ground.

But eventually, there was trouble in bird paradise. First the Maori came. The giant moa, a huge bird that looked something like an ostrich, was an excellent source of meat and eggs. The moas were so easy for hunters to catch that soon they were extinct. Some Maori brought dogs to the

Opposite: **Towering fern trees fill the thick forests of New Zealand.**

islands, and rats hitched rides there in the canoes. The Maori, dogs, and rats all feasted on bird eggs. By the time the first Europeans arrived, a third of New Zealand's 106 bird species had disappeared.

The European settlers brought cats, rabbits, weasels, and hedgehogs. Some of these animals ate eggs and birds. Others competed with the birds for food. The birds lost habitat as more forest was cleared to make farmland. Soon, half of the birds of Aotearoa were extinct.

A Variety of Birds

Because of New Zealand's unique location, many bird species exist only there and nowhere else in the world. Songbirds include the rifleman, the tui, and the hihi. New Zealand's many seabirds include five kinds of albatrosses, two kinds of skuas, and the Australasian little grebe. Like the rest of the

What Is a Kiwi?

a. A fuzzy, round brown bird
b. A fuzzy, round brown fruit
c. A person born in New Zealand
d. A New Zealand dollar

Of course, the answer is all of the above. The kiwi bird, which lives only in New Zealand, is the national bird. When New Zealand farmers developed a new fruit that was brown and fuzzy like the kiwi, they named it after the bird. Kiwi is also a nickname for a New Zealander. The dollar coin in New Zealand features an image of the kiwi bird, so it has become known as a kiwi.

Blue penguins are the smallest species of penguin.

world, Aotearoa also has many varieties of pigeons, swans, owls, and larks.

Several kinds of penguins live in New Zealand. Among them are the yellow-eyed, the Fiordland crested, and the blue penguin, also called the little fairy penguin. All make their home in the hillsides and cliffs above the sea. Fairy penguins are only 1 foot (30 cm) tall. They go out to sea for a few days or weeks at a time. Tourists and locals visit beaches south of Dunedin at sunset or dawn to watch the penguins surf in on the waves and waddle up to their nests to feed their young chicks.

Back from Extinction

Today, strong protection and breeding programs have been developed to help some endangered New Zealand bird species. The flightless kakapo, the heaviest parrot in the world, has a strong beak that it uses to climb trees. It glides to the ground

The kakapo is also known as the owl parrot because it has a sturdy body and round face, as do owls.

by spreading its weak wings like a parachute. All the remaining kakapos were transferred to an uninhabited, predator-free island where scientists watch over the birds. The scientists provide a special enriched diet to encourage the females to lay more eggs. They then take a few of the eggs from the nests and hatch them in incubators where they are kept warm. Because of this program, the population of kakapos has grown from fifty-one birds in 1995 to ninety-one in 2010. The takahe is another flightless, almost extinct bird, now under similar protection on a different island.

On Great Barrier Island off the North Island, the private estate of a bird lover has been converted into a bird sanctuary. Using a rodent-proof fence to protect it, the Glenfern Sanctuary has become a haven for native birds like the black petrel, the pateke (brown teal), the kaka, and the North Island robin.

Insect Life

A unique insect in New Zealand is the weta, which is similar to a giant cricket. There are about seventy different kinds of wetas. The tree weta eats leaves, seeds, and fruit. Wetas are nocturnal and flightless. If threatened, they wave their hind legs in the air as a warning to other creatures to stay away. They can scratch with their spiky legs and bite. The bite is painful, but not poisonous. The giant weta grows to be about 8 inches (20 cm) long, making it the largest insect in the world.

The Maori word for the giant weta is *wetapunga*, which means "god of ugly things."

Ancient Life

For years, most scientists thought that Aotearoa was too cold for dinosaurs to have lived there. That changed in 1975, when a woman named Joan Wiffen made an important discovery. She had read an article about Te Hoe, a mountainous area about 70 miles (110 km) inland that was once along the coast on the North Island. She thought it would be a good place to take her family to look for shells and fossils. When they cracked open a rock and found a unique bone inside, she knew what she was looking at: a dinosaur bone. It turned out to be an unknown species similar to *Tyrannosaurus rex*. Scientists have continued searching for dinosaur fossils in New Zealand, and they have now found bones from six species.

Another strange New Zealand insect is the glowworm. The glowworm is the larval stage of the fungus gnat. It lives in dark, moist areas like caves. To get its prey, its glowing body attracts insects, which then get caught in a long, sticky thread that the glowworm has released. The glowworm then reels in the thread and eats its dinner.

Sea Life

The ocean plays a large role in Kiwi life. The cold currents from the south mix with the warm currents from the north, encouraging abundant growth of tiny organisms called plankton. Plankton is the basis of the food chain for most sea life. Species such as snapper, trevally, tarakihi, and kowhai are fished both commercially and for sport. Sea stars, jellyfish, mussels, barnacles, and oysters also thrive in these waters.

Twenty-two different kinds of whales live offshore, either year-round or during breeding season. To help protect the whales, hunting is illegal in all New Zealand waters. New Zealand has also established eighteen sanctuaries where people can swim, boat, and snorkel, but not harvest animals. After whaling, collisions with large ships are one of the biggest threats to whales. This happens several times a year in New Zealand waters. Efforts are being made to create a thermal imaging system to spot surfacing whales sooner and give captains of large ships time to change course.

Deep ocean trenches lie not far off the coast of New Zealand, so unusual sea life occasionally washes up on the shore. Scientists come immediately when people find animals like the giant squid or the oarfish, which looks a bit like a surfboard and swims vertically. They hope to learn more about sea life in the deep trenches.

Humpback whales often jump completely out of the water. Scientists think they do this for fun, to clean pests off their skin, to communicate with other whales, or to show off.

Symbols of the Nation

The kiwi and the silver fern are the most important national symbols of New Zealand. Both were first used as symbols on the badges of some New Zealand troops in the late 1800s and are now used as logos for the country.

The kiwi is the best known of the flightless birds of New Zealand. The North Island brown kiwi is the most common of the five species of kiwis. It is about the size of a football and has little legs and a long curved beak. The kiwi is nocturnal, coming out of its burrow at dusk to search the ground for insects and worms. It has poor eyesight but a great sense of smell, with its nostrils on the end of its beak. The small bird digs in the ground with its beak, following its nose to find a meal.

The cool, wet forests of New Zealand are rich with ferns, some of which grow as tall as trees. In the spring, the round, coiled sprout of a frond is both welcome food and a symbol of new life and hope. The silver fern tree looks like a cousin to a palm tree. The 12-foot-long (4 meter) fronds grow in a bunch on the top of the tall trunk. The tops of the fronds are a muted green, but underneath they are silver. Both the coiled frond and the fully opened frond of the silver fern represent the spirit of New Zealand.

The Ancient Forest

Eighty percent of Aotearoa was once covered with thick forest. Today, only about 23 percent of the land remains forested. Most has been cut for timber or burned to create farmland. The ancient forest was filled with species unique to Aotearoa. Some of the old trees are the great kauri, which can grow for two thousand years. The tree was highly valued by Maori looking for strong, straight trees to carve into oceangoing canoes and for European sailing captains looking for new masts to replace ones snapped off in storms.

New Zealand is a temperate rain forest. It gets large amounts of rain but has a cooler climate than a steamy tropical rain forest. It is a perfect climate for growing ferns. The largest is the black fern tree, which grows to 65 feet (20 m) tall and has a bushy group of fern fronds at the top of its long trunk.

Hikers stand before a giant kauri tree on the North Island.

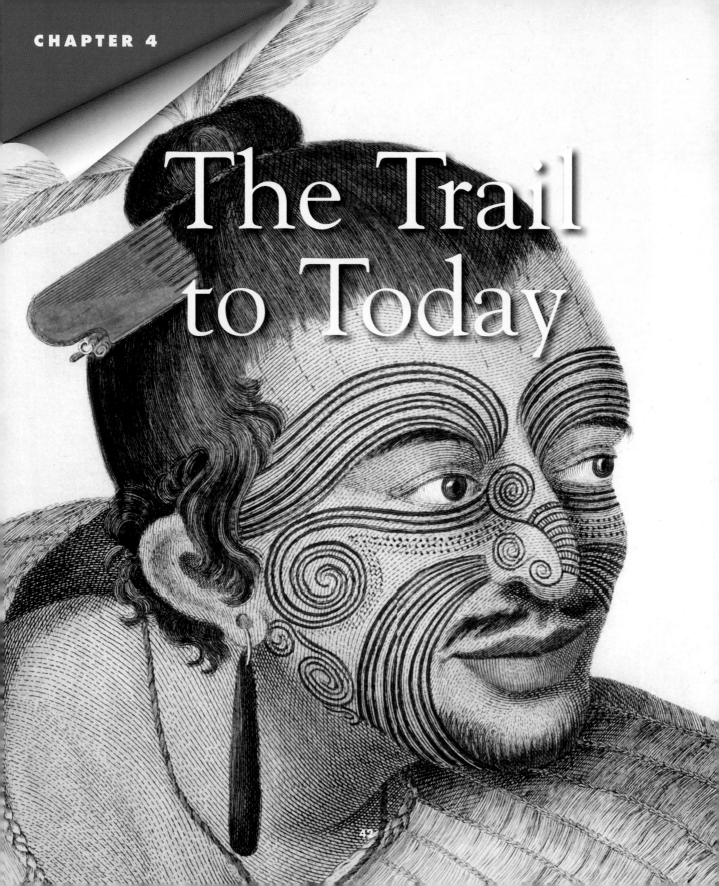

CHAPTER 4

The Trail to Today

THE FIRST MAORI LANDED IN AOTEAROA IN ABOUT 1280 CE. For five hundred years the Maori had Aotearoa to themselves. As different groups of Polynesians followed, they settled in different areas. The groups hunted and planted crops. They developed a strong culture rich in music, poetry, art, dance, and facial tattooing.

Europeans Arrive

The first European contact came when the Dutch explorer Abel Tasman was sailing along Australia in 1642. He was blown off course, got lost, and eventually sailed to Aotearoa. He anchored off the North Island and sent a landing party to the west shore to search for fresh water. The Maori thought the Dutch had come to attack and steal food. They performed a traditional warning dance called the *haka*. They then got in their canoes and attacked first, killing four sailors. Tasman and his crew fled and did not try to land on Aotearoa again.

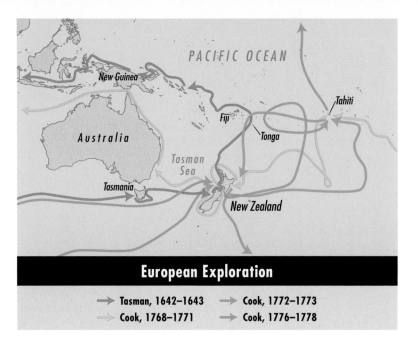

European Exploration

→ Tasman, 1642–1643   → Cook, 1772–1773
→ Cook, 1768–1771   → Cook, 1776–1778

After hearing stories of Tasman's journey, the following year other Dutch trading ships sailed down the east side of Aotearoa. They named it Nieuw-Zeeland after a province in the Netherlands.

In 1769, the British explorer James Cook visited Aotearoa on his first voyage around the world. More than one hundred years had passed since Europeans had visited Aotearoa. Traveling with Cook was a Tahitian leader and priest named Tupaia, who spoke the same root language as the Maori. They could roughly understand each other and developed friendly relationships and trade. While there, Cook made detailed maps of Aotearoa.

Sealers and Whalers

After Cook's first visit, things began to change for the Maori. As good information and maps became available, sealing ships headed south. They began arriving in Aotearoa in big numbers in 1792. In the decades that followed, more and more whaling ships arrived. After time at sea, the ships often used Kororareka, now called Russell, on the North Island as a place to rest, get supplies, and entertain themselves. North Americans from New England whaling towns were the largest group of foreigners in Aotearoa at this time.

At first, the Maori traded their food, water, wood, and other goods for cheap trinkets, but as more ships came for supplies, the Maori began demanding tools, alcohol, and muskets. Some Maori groups used their new muskets in battles with other villages. Thousands of Maori died in what were called the Musket Wars.

Disease brought by the outsiders killed even more Maori. Other Maori left to work on the ships and did not return. In the first fifty years of regular outside contact, the Maori population fell by half.

On his first voyage to the Pacific, James Cook claimed land in Australia and New Zealand for the British Crown.

Missionaries and Settlers

In 1814, a whaling ship docked at Sydney Harbour in Australia with two Maori sailors. The Reverend Samuel Marsden was impressed with their stories of Aotearoa. He gathered a group of twenty-one families to move there. These missionaries settled near Kororareka. When they saw the beautiful, rich land many quickly forgot about saving souls and started thinking about getting possession of that land. The Maori didn't understand the idea of buying and selling land. They thought land could be used by people for a time, but not owned by them.

Samuel Marsden preaching a Christian sermon to the Maori on Christmas Day, 1814.

As more missionaries and settlers came, they took more and more land from the Maori, sometimes for just a token payment.

At first, most Maori did not accept Christianity. Nor did they like the European farming methods the missionaries tried to teach them. The large horses that Marsden brought were frightening. The plows were unacceptable because the Maori believed the cuts hurt Mother Earth. The Maori didn't like the way many missionaries were disrespectful of their beliefs and of them.

More missionaries and settlers moved to other areas. A few missionaries tried to set up schools for the Maori and develop a written language for them. Before Europeans arrived, all Maori language and stories were communicated in symbols or the oral tradition, passed from generation to generation by memory.

Missionaries established schools in New Zealand, including this one in Waikato, on the North Island. At the schools, Maori people learned to read and also learned about Christianity.

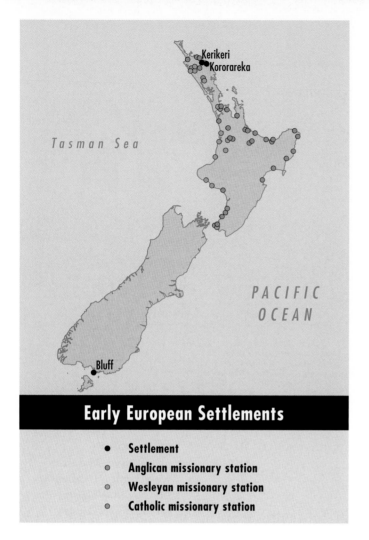

Early European Settlements

- ● Settlement
- ○ Anglican missionary station
- ○ Wesleyan missionary station
- ○ Catholic missionary station

Map labels: Kerikeri, Kororareka, Tasman Sea, PACIFIC OCEAN, Bluff

Another change the missionaries and settlers wanted was better order in Aotearoa. They asked the British to take possession of it. Whalers and timber merchants joined in the campaign for British control, because import taxes on whales and wood would decrease dramatically if New Zealand joined the British Empire.

The Treaty

Finally, in 1839 the British agreed to take over the land. First, they had to get the Maori leaders to sign a treaty recognizing the United Kingdom as head of the country. The missionaries convinced the Maori it was best for their people.

On February 6, 1840, many Maori leaders met with representatives from the British queen at Waitangi, on the North Island, to sign the treaty documents. The Treaty of Waitangi is the founding document of New Zealand, much like the Declaration of Independence is for the United States. Later, it was taken through the country and signed by over five hundred, though not all, Maori leaders. With that, Aotearoa disappeared and New Zealand took its place. It became Britain's most distant colony, on the opposite side of the globe.

There are three articles of agreement in the Treaty of Waitangi:

The first recognized the British Crown as head of New Zealand and allowed non-Maori people to settle there.

The second allowed the Maori to keep their traditional land and their culture. Maori leaders would retain their authority over the Maori people.

The third gave the Maori the rights of all British Commonwealth citizens.

At the ceremony there were two copies of the treaty, one in English and one in Maori. The translations were not the same, so each side had a different understanding of what it was agreeing to. For the Maori, it was the difference between

Maori leaders sign the Treaty of Waitangi in 1840.

surrender and forming an alliance, an equal partnership. This almost immediately led to disputes that continue today.

Land Wars Continue

Naval captain William Hobson became the first governor of New Zealand. He needed to raise money to run the new government. He bought Maori land at very low prices, whether the people wanted to sell or not. Then he immediately sold it to new settlers and land companies at much higher prices, often twenty times

Maori leader Hone Heke was an early supporter of the Treaty of Waitangi, but he soon became frustrated with British control over Maori affairs. Beginning in 1844, he and his men repeatedly cut down the British flag.

what he had paid the Maori. Between 1840 and 1850, the number of settlers went from two thousand to twenty-two thousand.

As the government forced the Maori to sell more and more land, they became ever angrier. Only the government was allowed to buy Maori land, but it was supposed to pay a fair price. Although this was meant to protect the Maori, it instead left them feeling cheated.

The Maori began to fight back, attacking British troops. In Russell, a young Maori leader named Hone Heke kept chopping down the British flagpole. He did this four times, even after the British wrapped the wooden pole in iron and put a twenty-four-hour guard on watch. Eventually, the British solved this problem by moving the capital from Russell to Auckland. Over the next twenty years, the Maori attacked the army and settlers who were taking their land.

In 1858, Maori leaders decided they would be more unified and better able to fight the British if they chose one person to be king. They crowned Potatau Te Wherowhero of the Waikato group king of the Maori. While hostilities still existed between different Maori groups, they became less important than fighting the British.

Most of the gold prospectors in New Zealand were Scottish, Irish, and English. Many had first tried their luck mining in Australia before sailing to New Zealand.

Gold Rush

In 1861, gold was discovered in the rocky creeks of the Otago area on the South Island. Word spread around the world and people rushed there to get rich. But the gold disappeared quickly.

In six months, the population of the nearby Canterbury Plains grew from thirteen thousand to thirty thousand settlers. Though the gold did not last, the region's natural resources proved valuable. The newcomers discovered that the plains and hillsides were great for raising sheep and cattle and that the trees could easily be cut and shipped to Britain. The settlers pressured the government to make more land available for farming and timber cutting.

As the Maori continued to lose their land, the Land Wars dragged on. Many soldiers, settlers, and Maori died. In time, the Maori became disheartened and the wars finally stopped in 1882. Before European contact, an estimated 120,000 Maori lived in Aotearoa. By the end of the 1800s, the Maori population was only 42,000.

In 1880, Dunedin was the largest city in New Zealand.

Keeping Things Cold

For years, people had been trying to find a way to ship frozen meat long distances. Live animals almost always died on the way. Packing big blocks of ice in sawdust to create cold compartments in the cargo hold worked for short distances, but New Zealand was too remote.

In 1882, a New Zealand sailing ship called the *Dunedin* tried a new system. An air compressor was installed on board. It compressed air by squeezing out the space between the molecules of air. The compressed air was piped into the ship's hold where it expanded again. As it expanded, it grew colder, lowering the air temperature 40°F (22°C). In cool climates like southern New Zealand, where the air temperature might be 50°F (10°C) before being compressed, the meat in the hold would freeze. As the air circulated through the pumps and compressor, the meat stayed frozen when the ship sailed through the tropics. It took 3 tons (2.7 metric tons) of coal a day to operate the steam-powered compressor.

When the *Dunedin* pulled into London ninety-eight days after leaving New Zealand, it had five thousand frozen meat carcasses, 250 kegs of frozen butter, and many frozen chickens, pheasants, and turkeys. A rush began to build many more refrigerator ships, or reefers as they were nicknamed. A new industry was born.

By the 1880s, wool and timber were New Zealand's main exports. The invention of refrigerated cargo ships in 1882 opened markets for New Zealand meats and dairy products around the world.

Becoming Independent

Unlike other colonies in the British Empire, New Zealand never had to fight England for new rights or independence. Rights were requested and granted, sometimes slowly and sometimes immediately. In 1852, New Zealand was given the right to form its own parliament with an elected House of Representatives and a Legislative Council appointed by the queen or governor. New Zealand was granted responsibility for its own domestic affairs, but not for foreign policy or issues related to the Maori. Ten years later, the British government gave New Zealand the right to manage issues with the Maori, too. And in 1907, New Zealand was declared a dominion within the British Empire, indicating that it was largely self-governing. In 1935, after New Zealand had participated in World War I, and many Kiwis had lost their lives, New Zealand demanded the right to make its own foreign policy. The British were not yet ready to agree, however.

Soldiers from New Zealand line up during World War I. One hundred thousand New Zealanders served in the war. At the time, New Zealand had a total population of just one million.

Rights for Women

In the late 1800s, women in New Zealand were worried about the lack of power they had. Led by suffragette Kate Sheppard, New Zealand women began a fight for their rights. More than thirty thousand women signed a petition to Parliament asking for the right to vote. In 1893, New Zealand became the first country in the world to grant women the right to vote. Today, Kate Sheppard is featured on New Zealand's $10 bill.

In 1947, New Zealand approved the Statute of Westminster, a law that made it a fully self-governing country. However, it wasn't until 1950 that the queen-appointed Legislative Council was abolished.

Boom Times

In the middle of the twentieth century, New Zealand's economy grew. Agriculture and trade expanded. More timber was cut to

Many new schools were built in New Zealand in the 1950s, including Spotswood Primary on the North Island, in the shadow of Mount Taranaki.

A bus rumbles down a street in Auckland in the 1950s. By the dawn of the twentieth century, Auckland had already become New Zealand's largest city, and it continued to expand quickly in the following decades.

help rebuild Europe after it was devastated during World War II. The nation's economy really boomed beginning in 1950, when the United States began buying huge quantities of wool to make uniforms and blankets during the Korean War. As New Zealand prospered, the government showed commitment to giving its citizens a good life. It guaranteed a minimum wage, rights for women and Maori, good health care, adequate housing, and an education. The government also banned discrimination and capital punishment. The environment became a major concern for the country. As part of environmental awareness, new programs were developed to replant forests and help endangered birds survive.

Many Maori began rediscovering their culture. They formed groups to study it and celebrate it. They turned to the government demanding their rights under the Treaty of Waitangi. This time the government was ready to listen, and the Waitangi Tribunal was established.

The Waitangi Tribunal

Promises made to the Maori in the Treaty of Waitangi were broken almost immediately. Maori men were denied the right to vote and to get loans to improve their farms because they did not own their land individually. The Maori protested government land confiscation shortly after the Treaty of Waitangi was signed, but there was little they could do about it. In 1867, Maori men were finally allowed to vote and four seats were set aside in the New Zealand parliament for Maori representatives.

But it wasn't until the 1970s, when the Maori pride in their culture became more visible, that the government began to face issues of broken promises and land that had been unfairly taken from the Maori. A tribunal to hear claims against the government was established in 1975. As a result of the Waitangi Tribunal, the government has returned some land to the Maori and paid them more appropriately for other land. The Waitangi Tribunal continues its work today researching claims and helping to reach settlements.

Keeping New Zealand Safe

In recent years, New Zealanders have been working hard to keep both people and the environment safe. They are working to expand green energy. Voters have mandated a ten-year hold on building new fossil fuel plants. These are plants that use coal, natural gas, oil, or other polluting fuels. Kiwis hope that in ten years green technology will have grown so much that renewable energy will have replaced fossil fuels.

New Zealanders want to make this switch for several reasons. Green energy does not run out, does not pollute, and does not produce methane, which is released by underground coal and has been the cause of many dangerous mine explosions. Such explosions occurred at the Pike River coal mine in 2010. The mine owners had not enacted safety measures that were required by law, and on the afternoon of November 19, a series of methane gas explosions killed twenty-nine men. In the seven explosions that have happened in New Zealand coal mines, 210 men have been killed. Coal production had already been decreasing by 2010, and the Pike River mine is no longer in operation.

Ties to the World

By the late twentieth century, New Zealand was forging a strong identity of its own. In 1966, France began testing nuclear weapons on two islands in the South Pacific. New Zealand protested this out of fear that the radiation might be a danger to its citizens. In 1985, a ship called the *Rainbow Warrior* belonging to Greenpeace, an environmental organization, was docked in Auckland, preparing to sail to the testing area as part of a protest. The night before it was to leave, the boat exploded and sank. French officials later took responsibility for the attack. New Zealanders were furious at the French and became even more committed to their antinuclear stance. In 1987, New Zealand banned from its waters all nuclear-powered ships or ships carrying nuclear weapons.

As New Zealand looks to the future, it is not looking to England. Instead, it is looking to Asia, to the South Pacific, and to Australia. China is becoming New Zealand's largest trading partner and is investing heavily in the country. These days, when the tourists get off the planes in Auckland, they are as likely to be speaking Mandarin, Hindi, or Spanish as they are to be speaking English. With optimism, Kiwis are moving forward in a multicultural world.

The Pike River Mine explosion was the deadliest mining disaster in New Zealand since 1910.

CHAPTER 5

Governing New Zealand

I N 1901, LEADERS IN NEW ZEALAND MADE A VERY important decision. Six other colonies on the continent of Australia had decided to band together and form their own commonwealth. They asked New Zealand to join them. The leaders of New Zealand said no. They would rather New Zealand be its own country than part of Australia.

Unlike the United States, New Zealand didn't have to fight to break the governing ties of the United Kingdom. Over decades, New Zealanders petitioned the British for their rights. Gradually, they were granted. In 1947, New Zealand became an independent country. The appointed governor general became a ceremonial position. A prime minister chosen by the party that got the most votes became the head of government. In 1950, New Zealand eliminated the appointed Legislative Council, and the House of Representatives became the governing parliament.

Opposite: **Queen Elizabeth II, the British monarch and the head of state of New Zealand, walks with John Key, the prime minister of New Zealand and the head of its government.**

Two Anthems

After the Treaty of Waitangi was signed, the British national anthem, "God Save the Queen," became the anthem of New Zealand. It remains one of New Zealand's two official anthems today. The other is "God Defend New Zealand." The lyrics come from a poem written by Thomas Bracken in the 1870s. A contest was held to provide music for the poem. John Joseph Woods won the contest, and the new song was first performed on Christmas in the city of Dunedin on the South Island in 1876. It became a huge hit and officially became a second national anthem in 1977. Today, it is used more frequently than "God Save the Queen." When it is performed, the first verse is usually sung in both English and Maori.

English lyrics

God of Nations! At Thy feet,
In the bonds of love we meet,
Hear our voices we entreat,
God defend our free land
Guard Pacific's triple star
From the shafts of strife and war,
Make her praises heard afar,
God defend New Zealand.

Maori lyrics

E Iohwa Atua,
O nga iwi matoua
Ata whakarongona;
Me aroha noa
Kia hua ko te pai;
Kia tau atawhai;
Manaakitia mai
Aotearoa.

Governing Documents

New Zealand does not have a constitution that sets the rules of government. Instead, it looks to governing documents such as the Treaty of Waitangi. Although the queen is no longer part of the government, the treaty is still considered the most important document in the country. Besides the treaty, New Zealand's governing documents are a series of laws called the Acts of Parliament. The first was the Constitution Act 1852, which the British Parliament passed to organize the New Zealand government. The Constitution Act 1986 made clearer all the laws passed between 1852 and then. To protect individual citizens, the Bill of Rights Act 1990 established the rights of people when dealing with the government.

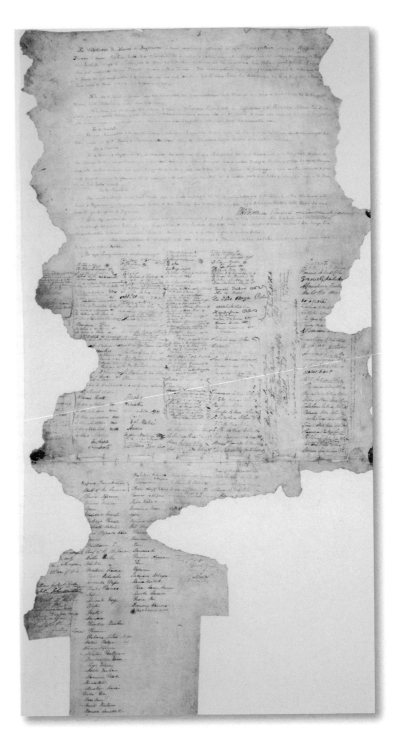

One of nine existing copies of the Treaty of Waitangi

Executive Branch

The formal head of state in New Zealand is the British monarch. He or she is represented in New Zealand by the governor general, but this position has very little actual power. The

New Zealand's National Government

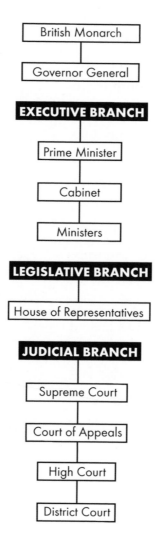

John Key worked in the banking industry before entering politics. He became prime minister of New Zealand in 2008.

head of the government is instead the prime minister, who is usually the leader of the party with the most seats in the parliament, called the House of Representatives.

The prime minister is assisted by a cabinet. The cabinet is made up of ministers who are in charge of different aspects of government policy. For example, there are ministers of defense, finance, tourism, science and innovation, and education. The prime minister is chosen from the cabinet. All cabinet ministers must be members of the House.

In New Zealand, every citizen and permanent resident over age eighteen is allowed to vote. Maori men gained the right to vote in 1867. All women were given the vote in 1893, but they were not allowed to serve in Parliament until 1919.

The voting rate in New Zealand is high, usually nearly 80 percent. About six hundred thousand Kiwis live abroad. Once they have been gone more than three years, they are no longer allowed to vote in New Zealand elections. The government assumes once they are gone that long, they don't know what is going on in the country.

Creating a Parliament

In New Zealand, when people head to the polls, each person gets two votes. One is for their local representatives. The other is for the party they want to control the government. There are two main political parties in New Zealand—the

National Party and the Labour Party. Many smaller parties are also active, including the Green Party, the United Party, and the Maori Party. Before the election, each party publishes a list of the people it will appoint as prime minister and to the cabinet positions if it wins. New Zealanders don't vote directly for prime minister, only for the party.

David Cunliffe is one of the leading members of the Labour Party, New Zealand's second-largest party.

The number of members in the parliament (MPs) varies from election to election. After people vote, the local rep-resentatives are chosen. If a minor party does not get a local seat but gets at least 5 percent of the overall vote, it is given a seat. All parties are given seats to match their percentage win. The Maori party also gets seats. Currently, the House has 122 members. Of this total, 63 are general members elected from their district, and 7 are Maori seats.

Often, no party will have more than 50 percent of the vote needed to establish a government. In that case, the leading party forms a coalition with smaller parties. For example, Prime Minister John Key is the leader of the National Party, but his government also includes the United Party, ACT New Zealand, and the Maori Party.

The Court System

The New Zealand government includes a number of courts that handle crimes and disputes. Less serious crimes are handled in

King of the Maori

In 1858, the Maori were frustrated with the Treaty of Waitangi and their loss of land and power. They thought a Maori king would have the same status with the settlers as Queen Victoria and be able to help save their land. The Maori king does not necessarily represent all Maori people. Historically, he has represented two large groups—the Tainui and the Ngati Maniapoto.

The great leader Potatau Te Wherowhero was the first Maori king. He did not have the power to stop the British from taking land, but the position was important in uniting the Maori. Today, the Maori king holds no political power in the New Zealand government, but like the governor general, is widely respected and has ceremonial duties. The current king is Tuheitia Paki (right), who took over for his mother the queen when she died in 2006.

district court. More serious issues and appeals, or reviews, of lower court decisions are heard in High Court. In 2003, the court system was changed so that the final appeals and most important cases were no longer sent to the Privy Council in London, England. A Supreme Court was established as the highest court in New Zealand, and it now hears those cases.

New Zealand also has special courts that handle specific types of cases. These include family court, military court, and environmental court.

The Parliament building in Wellington is one of the most recognizable buildings in all of New Zealand. It is known as the Beehive because of its shape.

A Walk Around Wellington

Wellington, the capital of New Zealand, is crammed between volcanic hills and the harbor, which is a sunken volcano crater. Wellington has a wide mix of architecture. There are ornate Victorian structures as well as buildings in streamlined art deco, a boldly geometric style of design popular in the first half of the twentieth century. One of the most important and delightful contemporary buildings is the Te Papa Tongarewa/Museum of New Zealand.

Wellington, nicknamed Welly, is a charming city, full of coffeehouses, bookstores, restaurants, shops, parks, and waterfront walkways. It has world-class theater, symphony, and ballet. The city has gorgeous

botanical gardens, art galleries, and even a fountain with a sense of humor. The Bucket Fountain is a series of colorful buckets that cascade water from one to another. However, every now and then, a bucket will swirl around and toss its water at passersby.

Government is the most important part of the city's economy. Other important economic sectors are banking, education, and medicine. Wellington's population is well educated and has a higher income than populations of other cities in New Zealand.

Map — Wellington

0 — 1 mile
0 — 1 kilometer

- Town Belt Park
- United States Embassy
- Westpac Stadium
- THORNDON
- Wellington Harbour
- Parliament
- Parliament Building (The Beehive)
- Wellington Railway Station
- Supreme Court
- Canadian Embassy
- Wellington Botanic Garden
- Queens Wharf
- Frank Kitts Park
- Lambton Harbour
- Kelburn Park
- New Zealand Symphony Orchestra
- Maori Arts Gallery
- Te Papa Tongarewa (Museum of New Zealand)
- ROSENEATH
- Victoria University of Wellington
- Bucket Fountain
- Waitangi Park
- TE ARO
- Evans Bay
- Pukeahu National War Memorial Park
- Tanera Park
- Central Park
- Massey University
- Town Belt Park
- Maupuia Park
- Wellington College
- HATAITAI
- MAUPUIA
- Weta Workshop
- Prince of Wales Park
- Alexandra Park
- Hataitai Park
- Miramar Park
- BROOKLYN
- Wellington Hospital
- NEWTOWN
- MIRAMAR
- MacAlister Park
- Town Belt Park
- KILBIRNIE
- Wellington Zoo
- Wellington International Airport

Wellington

National Flag

The first flag of New Zealand was born out of a need for a ship's home port to be recognized at sea. The Maori chiefs designed a flag similar to the missionaries' flag in 1834. It was named the United Tribes flag. When the Treaty of Waitangi was signed in 1840, Britain's Union Jack flag became the official flag of New Zealand.

In 1902, the British ordered all colonies to redesign their flags using a blue background and the seal of the colony on it. New Zealand didn't have a seal. Instead, New Zealanders put a small Union Jack in the upper left corner to show their relationship to Britain. The flag also includes the four main stars of a constellation called the Southern Cross against a field of blue to indicate New Zealand's position on the globe.

Local Government

New Zealand is divided into districts, which are in turn divided into city or rural council areas. Each area elects its own mayor and council members. The councils handle local matters, transportation, and the environment. Some districts provide services like wastewater treatment and public libraries.

The local councils are independent of the national government, but they can't make laws that go against national law. They can levy their own taxes, though, to pay for the services they provide.

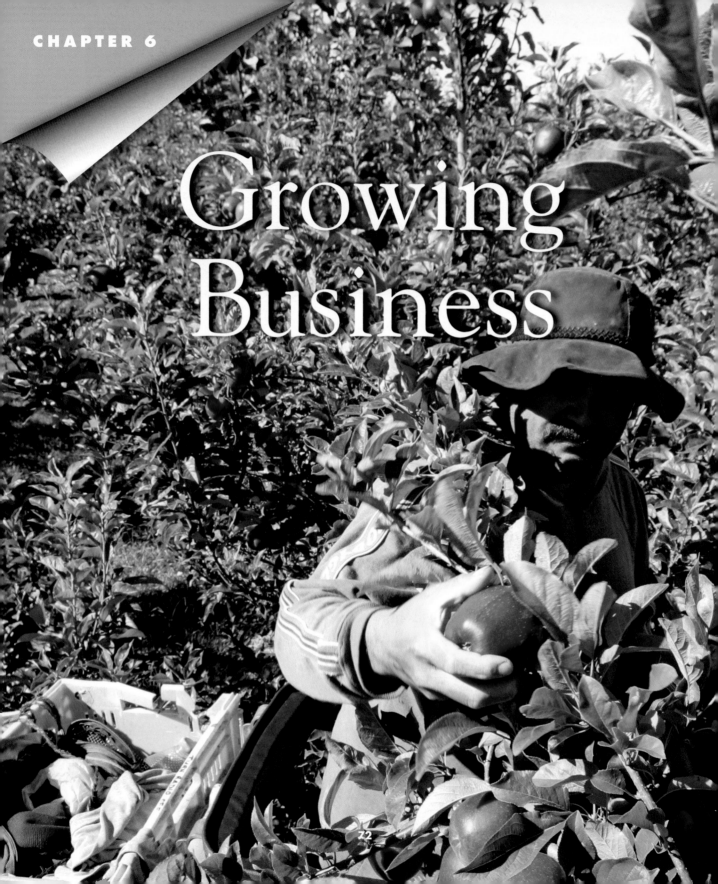

CHAPTER 6

Growing Business

WHEN THE FIRST MAORI PADDLED TO THE Aotearoa shore, they soon found that the land and coast could provide generously for people. Today, the land still provides for New Zealanders in two important ways. The land is good for ranching, and plentiful sun and rain allow many crops to be grown. Kiwis sell much of what they raise to other countries. The land also provides for the people by drawing tourists from all over the world to experience New Zealand's dramatic scenery and unique wildlife.

Opposite: **Royal Gala and Braeburn are the most common types of apples grown in New Zealand.**

Sheep, Cattle, and Beyond

For many years, New Zealand was the sheep and wool capital of the world. In 1980, there were seventy million sheep in New Zealand, more than twenty for every person. But then, new

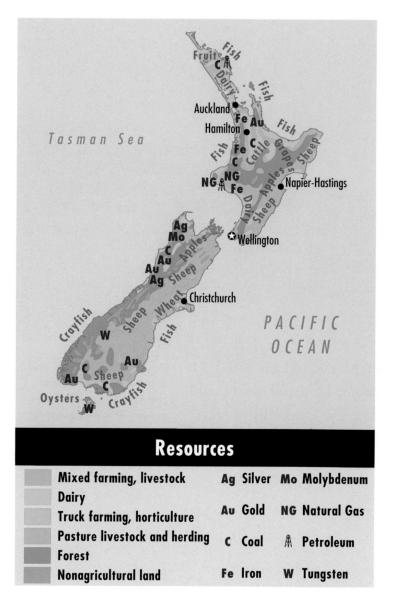

Resources

Mixed farming, livestock	Ag	Silver	Mo	Molybdenum
Dairy				
Truck farming, horticulture	Au	Gold	NG	Natural Gas
Pasture livestock and herding	C	Coal	⛏	Petroleum
Forest				
Nonagricultural land	Fe	Iron	W	Tungsten

synthetic fabrics were developed. As these fabrics became increasingly popular for clothing and blankets, the demand and price for wool fell. As a result, the number of sheep in New Zealand also fell. Today, New Zealand has ten sheep for every person. Wool remains in demand for carpeting, some types of clothing, and industrial uses, and lamb remains a popular food and export item.

Cattle have also been a longtime staple of the New Zealand economy. The quality of the cattle that is raised grazing on the volcanic grassland pastures is outstanding. It is also economical for farmers since they do not need to buy much supplemental food for the animals. Much of the cattle meat goes to the North American market.

New Zealand also has many dairy cows. The nation's number one export is dairy products, which includes cheese, butter, and powdered milk.

What New Zealand Grows, Makes, and Mines

A farmer herds sheep on the South Island. Lamb is one of New Zealand's most valuable exports.

AGRICULTURE

Sheep (2014)	29,800,000 animals
Cattle (2014)	10,400,000 animals
Potatoes (2013)	25,000 metric tons

MANUFACTURING (VALUE ADDED, 2009)

Food products	US$5,808,000,000
Fuels	US$2,069,000,000
Metal products	US$1,211,000,000

MINING (2012)

Hard coal	4,400,000 metric tons
Iron sand	2,395,000 metric tons
Gold	10,164 kilograms

Money Facts

The basic currency in New Zealand is the New Zealand dollar, which is divided into one hundred cents. New Zealand does not use pennies or nickels, however. All prices and change are rounded to the nearest dime. This saves the government from making lots of small coins, and people from having to carry them around. If, however, someone is paying electronically, as with a credit, debit, or gift card, the pennies and nickels are added and subtracted in the usual way.

Coins come in values of 10, 20, and 50 cents, and 1 and 2 dollars. A kiwi bird appears on the NZ$1 coin, which is nicknamed the kiwi. The kotuku, or white heron, is on the NZ$2 coin. Bills are printed in values of 5, 10, 20, 50, and 100 New Zealand dollars. The bills are made of polymer plastic and include a clear window that helps make them difficult to counterfeit. To make it easy to quickly tell the different bills apart, their size increases with their value. Each denomination of New Zealand dollar is also a different main color. The image on the front of New Zealand bills honors prominent figures in New Zealand history. A bird and a nature scene appear on the back. For example, the NZ$10 is predominantly blue, has a picture of women's rights advocate Kate Sheppard on the front, and shows a whio (blue duck) along with a river scene on the back. In 2015, NZ$1.00 equaled US$0.66, and US$1.00 equaled NZ$1.51.

Deer were originally brought to New Zealand in the 1860s for sport hunting. They thrived and soon spread across the country, damaging forests and pastures. Starting in the 1960s, farmers began capturing wild deer and fencing them into large pastures to raise them for their meat. The deer meat, or venison, is sold to restaurants and gourmet stores around the world. The antlers are sold to China for medicines.

New Zealanders raise goats for both their meat and their wool. Some farmers also produce wool by raising alpacas. These animals, which originated in South America, have extremely fine and soft wool, which is highly valued. Pigs and chickens are also important to New Zealand's economy.

A New Zealand beekeeper works with a hive.

In addition to land animals, New Zealanders raise fish and other sea life. Salmon is kept in fenced areas of the ocean. Mussels and oysters grow on racks submerged off docks in coves and bays.

New Zealand has a strong fishing industry. About 1,500 commercial fishing boats work in New Zealand waters. Snapper, tuna, trevally, cod, kowhai, squid, scallops, and lobsters are just some of what is caught.

Beekeeping is an important business in the country. New Zealand bees produce about 5,000 tons of honey a year. Several specialty kinds, including manuka honey, are believed to have healing properties and are popular in some Asian countries and in Great Britain.

Otago on the South Island is a major apricot-growing region. Most of the apricots are exported.

In Fields and Orchards

Because New Zealand stretches a thousand miles from the subtropical north to the cool south, Kiwi farmers raise a wide variety of foods. The Southern Hemisphere's growing season is the opposite of the Northern Hemisphere's, so New Zealand farmers can sell their goods to North America, for example, when few crops are growing there. In springtime in the United States, when apple trees are just beginning to bloom, markets are filled with freshly picked apples from New Zealand. New Zealand is famous for excellent apples, especially Braeburn and Gala.

Apples grow in orchards on the South Island, as do peaches, apricots, and cherries. In the northernmost reaches of New Zealand, citrus fruits like oranges and lemons grow. So do persimmons, passion fruit, and kiwis.

Kumara, purple-skinned sweet potatoes first brought to New Zealand by the Maori, are still grown, along with potatoes, pumpkins, and onions. New crops being raised for export include olives, macadamia and other nuts, and flowers.

As hillside pastures were no longer needed for grazing so many sheep, ranchers began planting them with grapevines. Soon, New Zealand was winning many international awards for its excellent wines. Hawke's Bay, Marlborough, and Central Otago are widely known for their world-class wines.

Rows of grapes grow at a vineyard on the North Island. New Zealand's wine production has increased quickly in recent years, and it is now one of the top wine-producing nations in the world.

Air New Zealand

One New Zealand business seen all around the world is Air New Zealand. It's easily recognized by the Maori koru symbol, twin silver ferns unfurling, on each plane's tail.

Air New Zealand started in 1940 with one floatplane. It was called the Tasman Empire Airways Limited (TEAL). It gradually added more floatplanes and routes. Floatplanes were used until 1960.

In 1965, TEAL changed its name to Air New Zealand and got its first jet. This enabled it to fly long distances to Europe, Asia, and North America. Today,

Air New Zealand is a worldwide airline that carries nearly fourteen million passengers annually. In 2015, Air New Zealand was ranked the best airline in the world. The airline is owned in equal parts by the government and private investors.

Timber

New Zealand has many timber farms where fast-growing pine trees are planted in tight rows so they will grow straight with a minimum of branches. After a few years, half the trees are cut and the rest are allowed to grow larger. It takes about twenty years to grow harvestable timber, but the trees can stay in the ground longer if there is not a good market for the timber. If the price and demand are high, the trees can be cut sooner. The largest market for New Zealand's logs is China.

Other Industries

Most manufacturing jobs in New Zealand involve processing food. There is also wood processing, oil refining, a chemical plant, a steel mill, and an aluminum smelter. A few other products, such as machinery and office furniture, are made for local use.

Tourism, information technology, and other service industries are major parts of the New Zealand economy. Many large international companies such as Microsoft have opened operations there to take advantage of New Zealand's well-educated and English-speaking population. Many local entrepreneurs are also starting their own technology businesses.

The film industry has long been important to New Zealand's economy. But director Peter Jackson has taken that to a new level of global involvement with Weta Workshop. This studio produced the hugely successful *Lord of the Rings* and *Hobbit* movie series.

The Weta Workshop created all of the figures for *The Lord of the Rings* movie trilogy.

High in the Sky

At 1,076 feet (328 m) tall, Sky Tower in Auckland is the tallest structure in the Southern Hemisphere. It was built between 1994 and 1997 as part of a downtown tourism complex. It is visible from all over the city and has become a symbol of Auckland.

At the top of the skyscraper are restaurants and observation decks. It also has a jumping platform for the fearless. The 630-foot (192 m) jump is attached to a cable to keep people from swinging into the tower. People can fall as fast as 50 miles per hour (80 kph) on the jump.

Sky Tower is also a telecommunications tower, broadcasting radio, television, and phone communications. In evenings it is lit, often with varying colors to promote charities, sports, or holidays.

Tourism

Tourism is the world's largest single industry, and New Zealand is doing a good job marketing itself as a top desirable place to visit. The traveling public's interest and curiosity are sparked by movies like *The Lord of the Rings*. Its Maori-British culture, amazing landscape, rare birds, and Kiwi fun and friendliness make New Zealand unique in the world.

New Zealanders see a strong link between protecting their natural resources and protecting their economy. Originally, whaling ships came to Aotearoa for hunting, rest, and trade. Before long, most of the whales were gone. Now, New Zealand has created whale sanctuary areas, and the whale population is growing. In Kaikoura, on the South Island, whale watching and swimming with dolphins are attracting tourists and revitalizing the area.

As world travel becomes increasingly more common, more and more hotels, hostels, shops, and restaurants open. Tourism is New Zealand's fastest growth industry, and the Chinese are the fastest growing group of tourists.

Interconnected

New Zealand is a part of the global economy. It trades goods with countries from around the world. Australia is New Zealand's number one trade partner. As China's economy boomed in recent years, its trade with New Zealand increased, and it is now the country's second-largest trade partner. Other major trade partners include the United States, Japan, South Korea, and the European Union. New Zealand imports goods such as oil, machinery, cars,

A Hangi and a Soak

Many tourists head to Rotorua, in the center of the North Island, to learn about the Maori culture and to have a good soak. This town of sixty-eight thousand, first settled by the Maori in 1350, is a center of Maori life and history. In Rotorua, the Maori have programs that teach about their history, culture, and celebrations. Tourists may attend a *hangi*, a feast that is traditionally cooked in the ground (left), and they can learn about the *haka*, a Maori war dance now done by the New Zealand national rugby team.

Rotorua is the site of geothermal springs and hot mud pools. The hot water that bubbles up from underground heats homes, is converted into electricity, and attracts tourists. The geothermal pools are filled with dissolved minerals. Many people think soaking in the minerals and heat is good for their health.

medical supplies, and food products. It exports dairy products, meat, timber, fruits, and other food products.

As New Zealand's economy grows and diversifies, the need for workers increases. There aren't enough workers for all the jobs in New Zealand. The country actively advertises for foreign workers to apply for skilled jobs. Salaries are increasing, especially for skilled entry-level workers.

Energy

It takes a lot of energy to keep the businesses, homes, and cars of New Zealand running. Luckily, New Zealand has a

Working for Antarctica

Christchurch is one of two places in the world that have a support station that helps scientists from around the world do research in Antarctica. From Christchurch it is a twelve-hour flight to Antarctica's McMurdo Sound, where the United States and other countries have research bases. The New Zealand research station is called Scott Base.

The first known person to visit Antarctica was a seventeen-year-old New Zealander named Alexander von Tunzelmann. He was working on a Norwegian whaling ship in 1895 when he set foot on the continent. However, it's possible other people went onto the land first, because other whaling and sealing ships were in the area.

Recently, Antarctica has become a popular tourist destination for the curious and the adventurous. During the summer, planes and ships leave from New Zealand to take visitors south for a taste of the coldest continent.

lot of natural energy, and New Zealanders are working hard to develop renewable resources. Much of the South Island uses hydropower from dams on fast-running rivers, although Kiwis hope to someday replace some dams with solar and wind power. The central North Island uses geothermal energy. New Zealand is installing wind turbines and tidal turbines, which work like underwater windmills. Currently, about 15 percent of the nation's power comes from wind. Solar panels are popular, and as they drop in price, more people are adding them to their rooftops. Currently, most of the North Island uses natural gas mined off Taranaki on the west coast of the North Island. The only energy that New Zealand imports is oil for use in vehicles.

Steam rises from a geothermal power station in New Zealand.

CHAPTER 7

Sharing Breaths

I F YOU ARE IN NEW ZEALAND AND SOMEONE HOLDS your shoulders, places his or her forehead against yours, touches noses with you three times, and your breaths mix together, you have just experienced a *hongi*. In the Maori culture, the hongi greeting demonstrates the human connection between people. The Maori believe that when you share breaths, you share lives. They believe everyone is an individual, but also part of a community, and that each person belongs to many communities: family, school, town, team. Sharing breaths shows that people belong to a shared community and are committed to one another. The hongi is often performed at special ceremonies, both political and civil, because it demonstrates the importance of partnership and the commitment of people to one another's lives.

Opposite: **Officials greet each other with a hongi at the opening of the New Zealand parliament.**

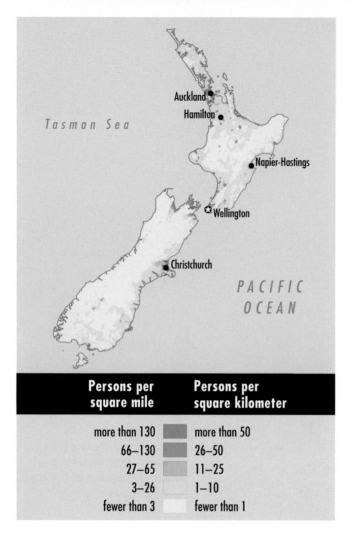

Persons per square mile	Persons per square kilometer
more than 130	more than 50
66–130	26–50
27–65	11–25
3–26	1–10
fewer than 3	fewer than 1

Population of Major Cities (2015 est.)

Auckland	1,454,300
Wellington	398,300
Christchurch	381,800
Hamilton	224,000
Napier-Hastings	129,700

Today, many Maori customs have become an important part of all New Zealand culture. New Zealand is an increasingly multicultural country, and the lives of all New Zealanders have mixed together like breaths. They are bonded into a strong community and a strong country.

Where People Live

New Zealand is thinner and longer than the U.S. state of California, but it has a population about the same size as the San Francisco Bay area. Two-thirds of New Zealanders live on the North Island. One-third of the people live in Auckland, which is about the same amount of people that live on the entire South Island.

People picture New Zealand as a peaceful countryside of sheep pastures and hillside vineyards. But in reality, 86 percent of New Zealanders live in urban areas. Big-city life and café culture are very popular in New Zealand.

New New Zealanders

Most New Zealanders have European backgrounds or Maori ancestry. When settlers began arriving in New Zealand in great numbers in the 1820s, British people were the most common

Before European contact there were about 120,000 Maori living on Aotearoa. Because of disease, disheartenment, and warfare, in the 1800s the number of Maori decreased to 42,000. Since then, many Maori have married people of other backgrounds, and today more than 600,000 people with Maori ancestry live in New Zealand. Another 150,000 Maori live elsewhere, mostly in Australia. Nearly 5,000 Maori live in North America.

group. Others came from Greece, Italy, and Germany. Today, New Zealand is becoming an increasingly multicultural country, with Asians the fastest-growing subgroup, made up of many Indians, Filipinos, and Chinese.

Asian restaurants are common in Auckland, the most diverse city in New Zealand.

Ethnic New Zealand (2013)*	
European	71.2%
Maori	14.1%
Asian	11.3%
Pacific Islander	7.6%
Middle East, Latin America, African	1.1%
Other	1.6%

*Total equals more than 100 percent because people were allowed to identify with more than one group.

Mount Roskill, a suburb of Auckland, has a large South Asian population.

New Zealand is a growing country. Each year the population grows by about a half of a percent. This is the result of a combination of having a higher birth rate than death rate and people moving there from other countries. More than a million of New Zealand's 4.5 million residents were born in other countries.

Besides births and regular immigration, New Zealand's population is increasing because of "temporary visa conversions." This is when a temporary visa holder applies for permanent residency. More people who come to New Zealand on a special temporary visa—such as a student visa—are staying, getting jobs, and becoming permanent residents.

Facial tattoos were once common among the Maori people.

Speaking the Languages

New Zealand has three official languages: English, Maori, and New Zealand sign language. When Maori became an official language in 1987 it gained the same legal rights as English. It is frequently used in ceremonies and government activities alongside English. Most Kiwis speak at least a few phrases of Maori.

Until the Maori cultural rebirth of the 1970s, the Maori language was almost dead, being spoken mostly by just a few elders. Now it is taught in many schools, including immersion schools where all instruction is in Maori. There are Maori language television stations, radio stations, newspapers, and Internet sites. Speaking Maori is an important part of Maoritanga, Maori culture.

Maori, like Hawaiian, is melodic. The alphabet contains only fourteen letters: all the vowels plus *h, k, l, m, n, p, r, t,* and *w. Ng* is also a separate sound combination. All consonants stand alone except *ng* and *wh,* but vowels can string after vowels. When speaking Maori, each vowel is pronounced separately.

A monument at Waitangi on the North Island contains writing in both Maori and English.

English the Kiwi Way

New Zealanders speak English with an accent closer to British pronunciation than North American. Kiwi English sounds midway between formal British English and casual Australian English. Like their Australian neighbors, Kiwis throw in lots of shortened words, nicknames, and fun twists. The capital city of Wellington, for example, is often called Welly. And words like *ay* are often used as placeholders or acknowledgments.

New Zealanders use the British form of spelling, for example, *harbour*, *labour*, and *colour*. And at the end of words, they reverse the *er* to spell *theatre* and *centre*.

In the United States, people go hiking. In New Zealand, it's called tramping.

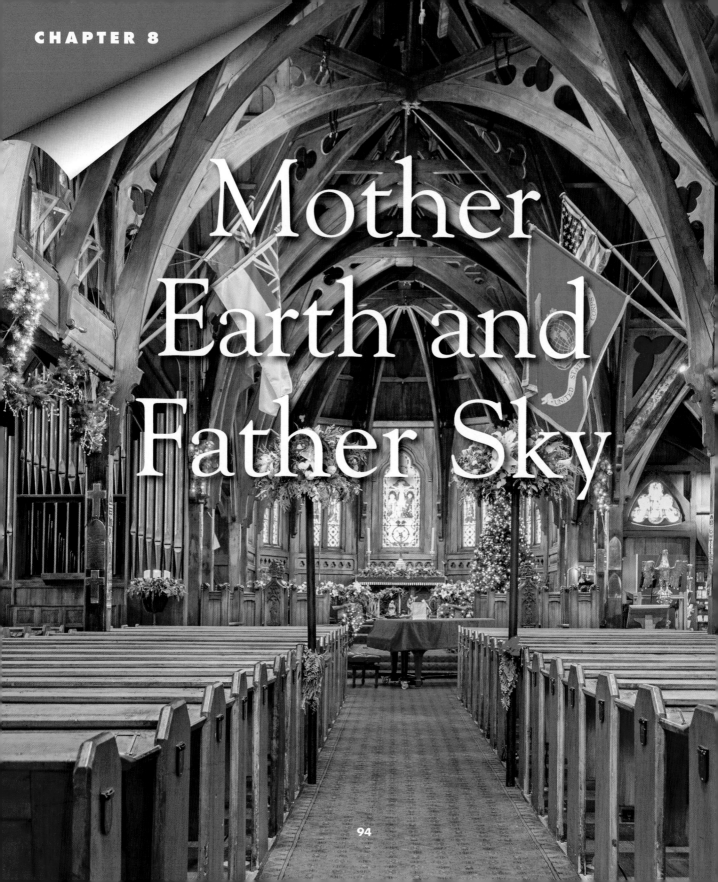

Mother Earth and Father Sky

WHEN THE MAORI FIRST ARRIVED AT AOTEAROA, they had strong spiritual beliefs. They revered Mother Earth and Father Sky and related to a forest spirit and an ocean spirit. They also honored their ancestors and held sacred the traditions carried from generation to generation.

Changing Beliefs

The most common religion in New Zealand is Christianity. The largest groups are Roman Catholic, Anglican, and Presbyterian. Since the 1960s, church affiliation has been falling rapidly. Today, more than four out of ten New Zealanders say they have no religious affiliation at all. Most people who do claim a connection to a particular faith say they do not attend services regularly.

Opposite: **St. Paul's was built as an Anglican church in Wellington between 1865 and 1866.**

Religion in New Zealand (2013)*	
Christian	48%
No religion	42%
Hindu	2%
Buddhist	2%
Maori Christian	1%
Muslim	1%
Other (including Jewish, Sikh, Baha'i)	1%
No answer	4%

*Total does not equal 100% because of rounding.

The Cardboard Cathedral

After Christchurch's stone cathedral collapsed in the 2011 earthquake, engineers decided that what remained of it needed to be demolished. The leader of the church, Reverend Craig Dixon, had to find a temporary place for church services. He settled on a site five minutes away and contacted disaster architect Shigeru Ban. Ban has won awards for his designs of temporary structures. For the church, he designed a new contemporary cathedral made partially of cardboard. With the city still recovering from the earthquake, it took two and a half years to complete and cost NZ$5 million.

The temporary structure has shipping containers for walls and a plastic roof. It is also made of heavy-duty cardboard tubes coated for water and fire protection, and laminated wood beams. The front wall is made of stained glass triangles. The building is shaped like a triangle, which is one of the strongest, most stable shapes there is. The beams and triangular roofline are reminiscent of a Maori marae (meeting grounds).

Besides church services, the building is used for community events, concerts, and meetings. Although it's named the Transitional Cathedral, Kiwis have nicknamed it the Cardboard Cathedral. It has become a new landmark in Christchurch, as popular to visit as the old Gothic cathedral.

As a country, New Zealand defends everyone's freedom to choose his or her own religion. In recent years, as the number of immigrants from Asia has grown, so has the variety of religions in New Zealand. Today, Hinduism is the second most common religion in New Zealand after Christianity, followed by Buddhism.

Maori Beliefs

When Christian missionaries first came to New Zealand, Christianity was slow to take hold among the Maori. For several decades the Maori remained uninterested. However, the missionary schools were an opportunity for them to learn to read and better understand Europeans. Eventually, many Maori converted and raised their children as Christians.

A dancer performs during Diwali, the Hindu festival of light, in Auckland.

In the Heart of Ancestors

Honoring ancestors is an important part of Maori belief. The heart of Maori community life is the marae, which is a center built to honor ancestors, tell their stories, and represent their good counsel. It is a place for celebrations, welcomes, mournful farewells, and meetings for discussions and learning. Long ago, the Maori believed that when ancestors died they would leave their wisdom and strength to their descendants. Their spirits would flow in their descendants' veins. The marae represents this belief.

The marae consists of several buildings, including the *wharenui*, the main meeting place. The wharenui is built to honor a specific ancestor of the group. This sacred place is always built with the same design. The front has

two side extensions like welcoming arms. Overhead is a strong center beam running the length of the building like a strong backbone. Exposed crossbeams represent ribs. The beams and columns are carved with stories and pictures of the ancestor's life. Inside the main room is like being inside the ancestor's heart.

To visit a marae, one must be invited. Certain movements, chants, and songs must be performed before entering the marae. The marae and the space leading to the buildings are sacred and are treated that way.

A board of trustees and a community of workers maintain the marae, keeping it in good condition. As more people have moved to cities, some marae have fallen into disrepair. But the Maori community as a whole is working to maintain the beauty and good feeling of all marae.

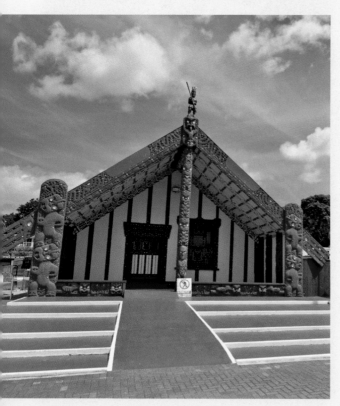

The interior of a church in the Maori settlement of Putiki is covered with Maori designs.

However, for some Maori, their traditional customs remained and became part of their Christian beliefs. This combination of beliefs is called Maori Christianity.

Karakia are Maori prayers or chants that are sung at special times. They are used to convey a wish for success in a coming event; a welcome to a newcomer; or to wish someone well as they leave. Karakia are poetic, with vivid imagery and a connection to nature. They are complex in meaning and often can't be properly translated into English. Traditional karakias are still performed, but with Christianity, new ones have been added.

Two Karakias

A Traditional Karakia

Cease the winds from the west

Cease the winds from the south

Let the breeze blow over the land

Let the breeze blow over the ocean

Let the red-tipped dawn come with a sharpened air.

A touch of frost, a promise of a glorious day.

A Christian Karakia

Honor and glory to God

Peace on Earth

Goodwill to all people

Lord, develop a new heart

Inside all of us

Instill in us your sacred spirit

Help us, guide us

In all the things we need to learn today

Amen

Church and State

New Zealand has a long-standing tradition of separation of church and state. But ties to Christianity from New Zealand's early missionary history have left New Zealand with some religious customs. The Christian religion and traditions can be taught in state-financed schools. Government meetings can be started with a prayer. Some Christian religious days are national holidays.

Overall, New Zealanders are respectful of religion, but a large percentage are not interested in formal religion. They find peace and spirituality in nature, in Mother Earth and Father Sky.

People in Auckland gather to celebrate the Jewish holiday of Hanukkah.

CHAPTER 9

Arts and Sports

THE CREATIVE ARTS AND SPORTS ARE HIGHLY VALUED in New Zealand. Besides being good for the Kiwi soul, arts and sports are good for the Kiwi economy. They are big moneymakers for New Zealand's tourist market. In many ways, a rugby ball is just as much a symbol of New Zealand as is the kiwi bird. And it makes Kiwis and visitors smile just as much.

Rugby

Although New Zealanders enjoy a variety of sports, rugby is at the top of the list. Most children begin kicking a rugby ball around the backyard shortly after they learn to walk. By age six, many begin playing on organized teams.

The New Zealand rugby treasure is the national All Blacks team. The All Blacks represent the entire country's passion and ideals. Wearing their distinctive black jerseys with a silver

The Best of the Best

Rugby legend Richie McCaw was born on New Year's Eve, 1980, in Oamaru, on the east coast of the South Island, where his family had a farm. It wasn't until he went to boarding school at age fourteen that he became passionate about playing rugby. In his last year of school, he was disappointed that he was not named to the national school team with future star players. Instead, he went to Lincoln University in Christchurch to study agriculture. There, he also determinedly worked on his rugby skills.

Soon, he became a player on the under 19s (years of age) national team. Suddenly, he saw that his dream of playing for the All Blacks might be reachable. With hard work, he became a substitute on the All Blacks team in 2001. In 2002, he was voted International Newcomer of the Year. By 2006, he had become the team captain. And, best of all, in 2011 he led the All Blacks to a World Cup championship.

Unfortunately, he has suffered several injuries along the way. But McCaw works as hard at physical therapy as he does at rugby and he has come back strong each time. Over the years, McCaw has won many awards and honors, including becoming the first international rugby player to captain one hundred games. He has been called the best rugby player that has ever lived.

fern logo, they do a Maori war dance, the haka, to intimidate their opponents before each match. Led by players like Richie McCaw and Dan Carter, the All Blacks have twice won the Rugby World Cup, in 1987 and 2011.

Rugby is popular with girls and women, too. The Women's Sevens team has an amazing record. (This type of rugby is called "sevens" because each team fields seven players instead of the usual fifteen.) The team won the women's international championship every year from 2010 to 2014.

The Fresh Sea Air

Rugby isn't the only passion among New Zealanders. On bays around the country, on Auckland's Hauraki Gulf, and on Lake Taupo, tall white triangles dance over the waves on most

Spectators gather to watch the beginning of a yacht race near Auckland.

breezy afternoons. Auckland is called the City of Sails, and sailboats large and small fill the harbor.

Many Kiwis take the America's Cup—the world's premier sailing event—very seriously. In 1993, Kiwis began secretly designing a new keel, the fin that extends below the boat, for their America's Cup entry named *Black Magic*. When other teams saw the new keel they filed protests, but the rules committee said innovation wasn't against the rules. *Black Magic*

Black Magic in action during the 2000 America's Cup

won the race in 1995 and again in 2000, and other countries hurried to create new designs of their own. Now marine engineers work with aerospace engineers and race car designers to build boats that are swifter and handle more easily. Today, the *Black Magic* boat hangs in the New Zealand National Maritime Museum in Auckland.

New Zealand reached the final of the Cricket World Cup for the first time in its history in 2015, but lost to Australia.

Having Fun
Cricket, which is similar to baseball, is New Zealand's most popular summer sport, both for watching and playing. The nation has recreational teams for everyone from young children to senior citizens.

Most Kiwis love to get outdoors. Kayaking is a popular activity.

Rarely do the summer and winter Olympics pass by without Kiwi athletes bringing home medals. Shot-putter Valerie Adams won gold in both the 2008 and the 2012 Olympics. She has won shot put events in the World Championship Games four times. Twins Caroline and Georgina Evers-Swindell won Olympic gold rowing the double sculls in 2004 and again in 2008.

Other New Zealand athletes have also made names for themselves. Ricardo Christie is a world-class surfer. Lydia Ko is a top golfer. She turned pro at age seventeen and became the youngest person to win an LPGA tournament.

In addition to competitive sports, Kiwis love recreational sports. They are always ready for a pick-up game of softball or to go fishing, kayaking, windsurfing, or horseback riding. Tourists love the big adventure activities of white-water rafting, bungee jumping, and skydiving.

Living with the Arts

In New Zealand, the arts are as much a part of people's lives as sports are. For many people, the day ends with a poetry gathering at a coffee shop, a walk through the city botanical gardens, a summer outdoor concert, or getting dressed up for the Royal Ballet. Each year, 92 percent of Kiwis are involved in the arts in some way.

If you are out for a hike along a lovely trail overlooking the sea or mountains, you are likely to come upon a person sitting at an easel painting the scene. If you begin talking, the person may say his mate is down on the beach gathering

New Zealanders gather for an outdoor concert on a warm summer day.

Te Papa Tongarewa/Our Place

At the edge of the sunken volcano harbor in Wellington stands a diverse collection of buildings joined together into a museum called Te Papa Tongarewa, Our Place, or the Museum of New Zealand. The museum opens windows into the history, geography, biology, culture, ideas, and values of New Zealand.

Te Papa Tongarewa is an interactive teaching place for young and old. Among its exhibits are simulators that let visitors ski a volcano or bungee jump off a bridge, a life-size computerized "sheep" that tests a person's shearing skills, and an earthquake house that regularly rattles visitors. There's a marae that visitors may enter to learn more about the Maori. On display is an authentic *waka* (canoe) that was recently carved from a kauri tree in the old way. The museum also houses a gallery of work by New Zealand artists, historical archives, research facili-

ties, and a collection of model skeletons of extinct birds. Outside, the bush gardens represent environments from all regions of New Zealand.

driftwood for a sculpture, or invite you to an art opening of a favorite glass blower. Living in nature as they do, Kiwis see art all around them.

Unique to New Zealand is the combining of Maori traditions and values in contemporary art. The Te Papa Tongarewa/Museum of New Zealand in Wellington has a collection of some of the country's best.

Public Art

Public art and sculpture are scattered all through New Zealand, both in obvious places and in surprising places. In downtown Auckland, crosswalks, manhole covers, and railing fences bow to the Maori ancestry with weaving patterns and

Mine Bay

After studying under Maori elder carvers for ten years, Matahi Whakataka-Brightwell set out to do a master works carving. He went to the west side of Lake Taupo, the land of his mother. There, he found the perfect canvas—a rock wall at the water's edge.

For the next four summers he and four assistants worked on a stylized carving of Ngatoroirangi, the great navigator who led Whakataka-Brightwell's mother's people to Lake Taupo. The carving is more than 30 feet (9 m) high. To honor Aotearoa's multicultural heritage, Whakataka-Brightwell also carved two smaller Celtic designs—one of the south wind and one of a mermaid—to show the European ancestry. He took no pay for his work and presented it as a gift to Lake Taupo.

To see these carvings, people must take a boat. The best way is to travel by kayak or canoe as the Maori did and sit at the base of the sculpture, with no sound but the songs of the birds and the breeze rustling the trees.

symbols worked into their designs. The Auckland Art Gallery, housed in an 1887 building, has an excellent European collection and a collection of the best New Zealand artists.

On the South Island overlooking the Canterbury Plains, ancient Maori drawings still decorate the cliff wall. At Mine Bay, on the far side of Lake Taupo, is a rock wall with a new carving in the old Maori tradition.

Artists All Around

There are many talented artists in New Zealand. Film actor Russell Crowe was born there and is part Maori. Martin Henderson, who is from Auckland, appears on the TV show *Grey's Anatomy*. Anna Paquin, who grew up in New Zealand,

Ta Moko

In traditional times, many Maori men had elaborate facial tattoos, called *moko*. Women had smaller tattoos on their lips and chin. The tattoos were painful and brought risk of infection. The tattoos were made by carving designs into the skin with bone knives. Charcoal or another pigment was then pounded into the cuts. The Maori believed that the more tattooing a man had, the braver he was.

The tattoos were fierce-looking in order to scare enemies. Many also told the story of the person who wore them. The person's family history was written in the swirls and symbols, telling what group he belonged to and often in which canoe his ancestors arrived at Aotearoa.

Today, most Maori wear temporary inked-on moko for celebrations and special occasions. But some young people are choosing to get traditional moko, often created in the traditional way. Most have the designs etched into their shoulders or backs. They walk in two worlds—one is of their Maori ancestors and the other is of their Kiwi life as a lawyer, actor, or businessperson.

captured the world's attention at age eleven when she won an Academy Award for Best Supporting Actress for the 1993 film *The Piano*. She has since appeared in films such as *X-Men*.

Many successful writers are from New Zealand. Katherine Mansfield's subtle and evocative short stories are studied in college classes. Keri Hulme won the coveted international Man Booker Prize for her 1984 novel *The Bone People*, which concerns an artist of mixed Maori and European heritage and

the wild little boy she befriends. Eleanor Catton won the same award in 2013 for *The Luminaries*, a lively tale set in the nineteenth-century New Zealand goldfields.

New Zealand has also produced renowned children's book writers. Maurice Gee has written many science fiction and fantasy books for young people, including *Under the Mountain* and *Salt*. Margaret Mahy also wrote books about the supernatural for young people, such as *The Haunting* and *The Changeover*.

New Zealand has an enthusiastic and varied music scene. The New Zealand Symphony Orchestra in Wellington, rock

At age twenty-eight, Eleanor Catton was the youngest person ever to win the prestigious Man Booker Prize.

Pure Heroine

From the time she was a young child, Lorde (born Ella Yelich-O'Connor) sang. She always knew she wanted to perform. At age thirteen, she and a friend won the school talent show and got invited to appear on the radio. This led to singing gigs in local cafés and at other events. She released her first recording for free over the Internet, and by age sixteen she had a hit record. Her first album, *Pure Heroine*, appeared in 2013 and was a hit around the world. The following year, she won Grammy Awards for Best Pop Solo Performance and Best Song of the Year. Her recording of the song "Everybody Wants to Rule the World" is part of the *Hunger Games* soundtrack. Lorde's music tends to be fairly simple, giving her mysterious voice plenty of room to express itself.

and reggae bands in Auckland, totally fun college bands in Dunedin, bagpipers in Christchurch, and buskers performing on street corners all over the country leave Kiwis humming and tapping their way down the streets. One of the most successful musicians in recent years is Lorde, whose song "Royals" catapulted her to international fame at age sixteen.

Using Imagination

New Zealand has become famous for being the location where *The Lord of the Rings* and *Hobbit* movie series were filmed. The movies, made by director Peter Jackson and Weta Workshop, became wildly popular around the world. Many people now come to New Zealand to spend time in what they know as Middle Earth, the setting of the movies.

Filming Middle Earth

Filmmaker Peter Jackson loved films from a very young age. When he was nine, a friend gave his family a film camera, and Peter immediately began shooting movies. He made up stories and got family and friends to act them out. At age twelve, he did a remake of one of his favorite films, *King Kong*.

After finishing school, Jackson saved all his money for camera equipment. In 1987, with the help of friends working for free on weekends, he wrote, directed, and produced *Bad Taste*, a movie about aliens coming to Earth planning to use people as food. The film was a hit at the Cannes Film Festival in France.

This led to several other projects including *Heavenly Creatures*, for which he earned his first Academy Award nomination, for Best Screenplay. With friends, he established a film studio in Wellington called Weta Workshop and surrounded himself with a loyal and talented group of coworkers. Together, they produced the phenomenally successful *Lord of the Rings* trilogy, bringing the world of Middle Earth to life. Today, Jackson continues to make his home near Wellington and prefers to film in New Zealand. Weta Workshop designs and produces sets, characters, and technology for projects from around the world.

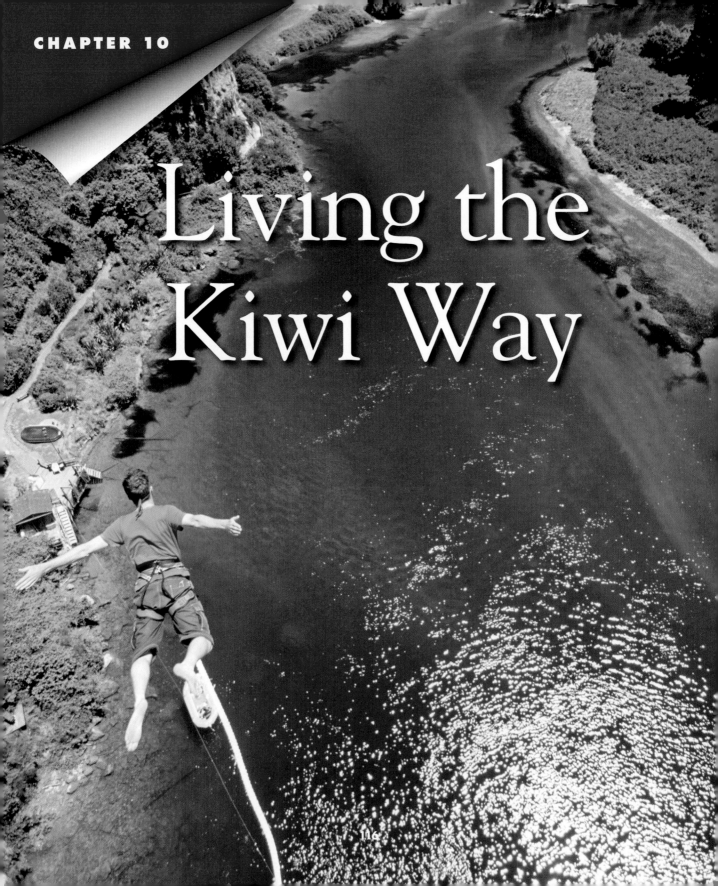

CHAPTER 10

Living the Kiwi Way

NEW ZEALANDERS ARE WELL KNOWN FOR THEIR friendliness and fun attitude, but there is much more to the country's culture. The histories of New Zealand and North America have some things in common. Almost all of the people who live there now, or their ancestors, made a decision to leave their old lives behind. They decided to go somewhere else and build a new life in a new land. The people were willing to take risks and work hard; traits that continue to serve New Zealand well. The people are inventive, thoughtful, and take action to get things accomplished, both individually and as part of a community.

Many groundbreaking accomplishments have been made by New Zealanders. Ernest Rutherford, a Nobel Prize–winning physicist, was the first person to split the atom. Sir Edmund Hillary and his guide, Tenzing Norgay, were the first people

Opposite: **Bungee jumping is popular in New Zealand. In bungee jumping, a person connected to a long elastic cord jumps off a bridge or other tall structure. The bungee jumper bounces up and down with the cord until it stops stretching and retracting.**

to make it to the top of Mount Everest, the world's highest peak. Electric fencing, refrigerator shipping, and the electric gasoline pump were all invented in New Zealand. All New Zealanders benefit from the national culture of adventure, innovation, and hard work.

Day to Day

The vast majority of New Zealanders live in towns and cities. They attend schools and work in businesses large and small. But Kiwis put a twist on the routines of daily life. There seems to be a national philosophy to keep life in balance, to work hard, and then to have plenty of fun. There's always time for a walk or a beach picnic. Workdays seldom go into the evening. Most shops close by six. Evenings are kept free for enjoying family, sports, and entertainment.

National Holidays

New Year's Day	January 1
Day after New Year's Day	January 2
Waitangi Day	February 6
Good Friday	March or April
Easter	March or April
Easter Monday	March or April
ANZAC Day	April 25
Labour Day	October
Christmas Day	December 25
Boxing Day	December 26
King or Queen of England's Birthday	

Honoring the Fallen

In World War I, New Zealand fought alongside the United States and Great Britain against Germany and its allies. When World War II began in September 1939, New Zealand became one of the first countries to declare war on Germany. During World War II, Kiwis worried that Japan might invade their country. Because New Zealand's soldiers were fighting throughout the Pacific, American soldiers went to New Zealand to help protect the country.

The heavy loss of life during the wars left deep scars on New Zealand. Australia New Zealand Army Corps (ANZAC) Day is celebrated each year on April 25, the day of a particularly deadly World War I battle in Turkey. The one-hundredth anniversary of the first ANZAC Day was celebrated in 2015 with ceremonies, visits to gravesites and battle sites, and a parade of World War I vintage vehicles owned by movie producer Peter Jackson. Stores and schools are always closed on ANZAC Day.

Kiwis are known for a relaxed, "no worries" attitude and a love of the outdoors. They are always eager to "have a go at it," whether it is a pick-up game of rugby, a sail on a beautiful afternoon, or a tramp in the misty mountains.

It's a Good Day for...

Most days involve outside activity for most Kiwis. Because New Zealand is an island, children are taught water safety and swimming at an early age. Surfing, sailing, kayaking, and fishing quickly follow.

Children ride bicycles along Lake Dunstan on the South Island.

Afternoons and evenings are often filled with team sports; rugby, cricket, and soccer are Kiwi favorites. But lawn bowling participants outnumber those in all other sports. Most lawn bowlers tend to be from the older generation.

Students may bicycle or skateboard to school, but unless they travel on one of the cycle paths, they must follow all the same rules as cars. They must stop at every stop sign, use hand signals for every turn, and always wear their helmets.

School in New Zealand

In New Zealand, a child's fifth birthday is a big day. On that day, children can start school. They don't have to wait for a new school year.

The school year is divided into four terms, each lasting about ten weeks. The first term starts in February. At the end of terms 1, 2, and 3, students get a two-week break. After term 4 is the long summer break lasting six weeks, from mid-December to the end of January.

New Zealand is known for its good schools. The literacy rate for the country is 99 percent. Besides learning to read, students study math, science, technology, language, social sciences, art, and physical education and health. In addition to academics, students learn social skills and how to compromise, analyze, and problem solve. Maori history and language are taught to everyone. There are also special Maori immersion schools where classes are taught in Maori.

Children have a basketball lesson at their school in Richmond on the South Island.

Students stay in school for about eleven to thirteen years, or at least until they reach their sixteenth birthday. At the end of that year, they receive a basic high school certificate. They can go into trade school or spend another year or two studying college prep courses called university. After finishing, they may choose to go to the University of Auckland, Massey University, the University of Otago, or any of the eight universities in New Zealand. However, many students are eager to experience the world and choose to study abroad.

The University of Otago in Dunedin is New Zealand's oldest university.

Kiwi Travelers

Kiwis are great travelers. Throughout the country are inexpensive hostels for backpackers or those touring the country by car. They are basic accommodations, but usually provide cooking facilities and lots of comradeship and advice.

Outside of the largest cities, most roads in New Zealand are two lanes and have light traffic. Rural bridges are often one lane. Large ferries connect the North Island and the South Island. Smaller ferries go to Stewart Island and other smaller islands. Traffic does not move fast up and down the length of New Zealand. The speed limit is generally 60 miles per hour (100 kph). It is the relaxed Kiwi philosophy to enjoy the ride and not rush.

New Zealanders are always happy to take time off and "jump the ditch" to travel to Australia, or go up to New Caledonia or Fiji.

A backpacker treks through the mountains at Fiordland National Park.

Shoppers pick out fresh produce at a market in Auckland.

Between finishing high school and establishing a career, many young people do an overseas experience, or OE. They save money and travel and work abroad from a few months to a few years. Many get jobs teaching English in Japan or China. When they return home to New Zealand it is with a broader understanding of the rest of the world and with global skills that help them work in New Zealand's increasingly global marketplace.

Eating Well

The quality of New Zealand meats and produce is high. In this country where the main exports are meat, fish, milk products, and fruits and vegetables, you would expect New Zealanders to eat well. And they do.

New Zealanders tend to eat more fresh produce and far less processed food than Americans do. Home gardens and fruit trees are in backyards all over town. Saturday and Sunday are farmers' market days. Corner produce markets are open almost every day.

Kiwis have left behind the British staples of boiled meat, boiled potatoes, and boiled peas. With the wave of increased Asian immigration, which started in the 1970s, came new ways of cooking. New Zealand has developed a wonderful local cuisine they call Pacific fusion. It's the coming together of fresh Pacific Island foods, Asian foods and cooking methods, and British standards. This is done in a way to create exciting new tastes using the freshest local foods. A piece of

Fish and seafood are popular in New Zealand cuisine.

Pumpkin Soup

Pumpkin soup is a New Zealand classic that has descended from the cooked sweet potatoes (kumara) first brought to New Zealand by the Maori. There are many different ways of making it that range from pumpkin broth to a hearty pumpkin stew. Here is a creamy version. Have an adult help you with this recipe.

Ingredients

1 large onion, diced

Butter

2 apples, peeled and diced

4 cups chicken broth or water

Salt and white pepper to taste

½ teaspoon nutmeg

2 pounds cooked pumpkin
  (or one large can)

¼ cup cream

Toasted pumpkin seeds

Fresh parsley

Directions

In a soup pot, cook the diced onion in a little butter for about five minutes over low heat. Add the apples and stir for about a minute. Add the liquid and spices. Add the pumpkin and stir. Then cook the mixture for 30 minutes. Adjust the spices to taste. Pour the mixture into a blender and blend until smooth. Pour the mixture back into the soup pot and reheat. Serve with a swirl of cream and toasted pumpkin seeds or a few fresh parsley leaves on top.

Kiwis relax at an outdoor café. New Zealand has become known for its comfortable restaurants and coffee shops.

lamb is no longer boiled. It might be sautéed in a lemongrass olive oil and glazed with spicy passion fruit sauce. It could be served with a local barley hazelnut pilaf and a sauté of baby zucchini and cherry tomatoes topped with fresh garden basil. Local chefs love competing with one another to come up with the most creative dishes in appearance and flavors.

Leading the Way

New Zealand honors its past, but it is also working to lead the world to the future. Dedicated to equality and committed to human rights, New Zealand was the first country to give women the right to vote. In 2013, New Zealand became the first Asian Pacific country to legalize same-sex marriage. New Zealanders believe decent health care, homes, and schooling are human rights. And they believe in taking care of Aotearoa. Kiwis want to look at the forested land and the sea rich with life and say, "Yes, this is a good land indeed."

Kia Ora, New Zealand. Kia Ora.

Timeline

The first Polynesians settle in Aotearoa. ca. 1280 CE

Dutch explorer Abel Tasman leads the first group of Europeans to reach Aotearoa. 1642

British explorer James Cook maps Aotearoa. 1769

Sealing ships begin arriving in Aotearoa in large numbers. 1792

Different groups of Maori fight each other in the Musket Wars. Early 1800s

The first missionaries arrive in New Zealand. 1814

The British and Maori sign the Treaty of Waitangi, giving the British control over New Zealand. 1840

WORLD HISTORY

ca. 2500 BCE	The Egyptians build the pyramids and the Sphinx in Giza.
ca. 563 BCE	The Buddha is born in India.
313 CE	The Roman emperor Constantine legalizes Christianity.
610	The Prophet Muhammad begins preaching a new religion called Islam.
1054	The Eastern (Orthodox) and Western (Roman Catholic) Churches break apart.
1095	The Crusades begin.
1215	King John seals the Magna Carta.
1300s	The Renaissance begins in Italy.
1347	The plague sweeps through Europe.
1453	Ottoman Turks capture Constantinople, conquering the Byzantine Empire.
1492	Columbus arrives in North America.
1500s	Reformers break away from the Catholic Church, and Protestantism is born.
1776	The U.S. Declaration of Independence is signed.
1789	The French Revolution begins.

NEW ZEALAND HISTORY

The Maori begin fighting Land Wars to try to stop land being taken from them.	**1840s**
The Maori crown their first king.	**1858**
Gold is discovered in the Otago region.	**1861**
Maori men are given the right to vote.	**1867**
New Zealand becomes the first country to grant women the right to vote.	**1893**
New Zealand becomes a self-governing country within the British Commonwealth.	**1907**
New Zealand becomes a fully independent country.	**1947**
The Waitangi Tribunal is established to hear Maori land claims against the government.	**1975**
France bombs the *Rainbow Warrior*, a ship involved in protesting French nuclear weapons testing, while it is docked in Auckland.	**1985**
New Zealand bans all nuclear-powered or nuclear-armed ships from its waters.	**1987**
Twenty-nine people are killed in the Pike River mine explosion.	**2010**
An earthquake hits Christchurch, killing 185 people and destroying much of the city.	**2011**

WORLD HISTORY

1865	The American Civil War ends.
1879	The first practical lightbulb is invented.
1914	World War I begins.
1917	The Bolshevik Revolution brings communism to Russia.
1929	A worldwide economic depression begins.
1939	World War II begins.
1945	World War II ends.
1969	Humans land on the Moon.
1975	The Vietnam War ends.
1989	The Berlin Wall is torn down as communism crumbles in Eastern Europe.
1991	The Soviet Union breaks into separate states.
2001	Terrorists attack the World Trade Center in New York City and the Pentagon near Washington, D.C.
2004	A tsunami in the Indian Ocean destroys coastlines in Africa, India, and Southeast Asia.
2008	The United States elects its first African American president.

Fast Facts

Official name: New Zealand (Aotearoa in Maori)

Capital: Wellington

Official languages: English, Maori, New Zealand sign language

Wellington

National flag

Southern Alps

National anthems:	"God Save the Queen," "God Defend New Zealand"
Official religion:	None
Government:	Constitutional monarchy
Head of state:	British monarch
Head of government:	Prime minister
Area of country:	104,454 square miles (270,535 sq km)
Latitude and longitude of geographic center:	41°S, 174°E
Bordering countries:	None
Length of coastline:	9,404 miles (15,134 km)
Highest elevation:	Mount Cook, 12,218 feet (3,724 m) above sea level
Lowest elevation:	Sea level along the coast
Largest lake:	Taupo, 234 square miles (606 sq km)
Longest river:	Waikato, 264 miles (425 km)
Average high temperature:	In Auckland, 74°F (23°C) in January, 59°F (15°C) in July
Average low temperature:	In Auckland, 59°F (15°C) in January, 52°F (11°C) in July
Wettest area:	Southern Alps, 250 inches (635 cm) of precipitation per year
Dryest area:	Central Otago, 12 inches (30 cm) of precipitation per year

Sky Tower

Currency

National population (2015 est.):	4,588,400	
Population of major cities (2015 est.):	Auckland	1,454,300
	Wellington	398,300
	Christchurch	381,800
	Hamilton	224,000
	Napier-Hastings	129,700

Landmarks:
- ▶ *Auckland Art Gallery*, Auckland
- ▶ *Sky Tower*, Auckland
- ▶ *Te Papa Tongarewa/Museum of New Zealand*, Wellington
- ▶ *Tongariro National Park*, Ruapehu District
- ▶ *Transitional Cathedral*, Christchurch

Economy: New Zealand's economy is based largely on food production and processing, technology, light manufacturing, and tourism. Meat, milk products such as cheese, wine, and fruits are all made for trade. Much of North America's lamb, hamburger, and venison comes from New Zealand. Trees are grown and processed into whole log timber and wood products for export. Wool and flax are raised and sold as yarn or textiles. Technology industries are growing quickly, especially in the entertainment field. Major movies, television, and special effects are produced in New Zealand. The nation's fastest growing industry is tourism, especially for adventure and nature travelers.

Currency: New Zealand dollar. In 2015, NZ$1.00 equaled US$0.66, and US$1.00 equaled NZ$1.51.

System of weights and measures: Metric system

Children

Lorde

Literacy rate:	99%	
Common Maori words and phrases:	*Kia ora*	hello
	E noho ra	Good-bye (from a person leaving)
	Haere ra	Good-bye (from a person staying)
	Haere mai	Welcome
	Ko wai tou ingoa?	What's your name?
	Ko . . . ahau	My name is…
	Kia waimarie	Good luck

Prominent New Zealanders:	Edmund Hillary *Mountaineer*	(1919–2008)
	Peter Jackson *Filmmaker*	(1961–)
	Lorde *Singer*	(1996–)
	Katherine Mansfield *Writer*	(1888–1923)
	Richie McCaw *Rugby player*	(1980–)
	Anna Paquin *Actor*	(1982–)
	Ernest Rutherford *Nobel Prize–winning physicist*	(1871–1937)

To Find Out More

Books

- ▶ Herman, Gail. *Climbing Everest.* New York: Random House, 2015.

- ▶ Morris, Sandra. *Welcome to New Zealand: A Nature Journal.* Boston: Candlewick Press, 2015.

- ▶ Theunissen, Steve. *The Maori of New Zealand.* Minneapolis: Lerner, 2003.

Music

- ▶ Lorde. *Pure Heroine.* New York: Lava Music, 2013.

- ▶ Te Runga Rawa. *New Zealand: Maori Songs.* Boulogne, France: Playasound, 2007.

▶ Visit this Scholastic Web site for more information on New Zealand:
www.factsfornow.scholastic.com
Enter the keywords **New Zealand**

Meet the Author

DONNA WALSH SHEPHERD IS BOTH A WRITER AND a teacher. She taught literature and writing at the University of Alaska–Anchorage for many years. She has written several books for Scholastic, including *Alaska*, *South Dakota*, *The Aztecs*, *Tundra*, and *Auroras: Light Show in the Night Sky*. She also writes articles and essays, mostly for adults. Shepherd has won several writing awards, but the best reward, she says, is to have a job where she continually learns new things, where she lives in awe and surprise at life and the world around her.

To research this book, she recalled her own visits to New Zealand and relied on Kiwi friends to advise her on current happenings and changes since she was last there. She read Web sites and contacted librarians both in the United States and in New Zealand. New Zealand's government Web sites were especially interesting and helpful. When not working, she often listened to audiobooks about New Zealand or by New Zealand authors. For Shepherd, writing this book was a welcome reminder that she must make a return trip to New Zealand soon.

Photo Credits